"It's hard to explain how much I've needed this book in my life. Sesshu Foster's coruscating *City of the Future* is a memory of Los Angeles spiked with expressionistic detail and a dissident's irreverence. Here, Foster offers no quarter to those who would destroy his community. But his profound generosity is abundant, especially for those who labor to make that community 'more livable for everyone.' Elegaic, documentarian, furious, and fun as hell, *City of the Future* is here to poke back at our thorny present. Take that, motherfuckers."
— DOUGLAS KEARNEY, *BUCK STUDIES*

"Sesshu Foster is the poet of the future: his work is encyclopedic, documentarian, but highly internal. Attuned to small incongruities and larger absurdities, Foster sees everything, from a police raid in Alhambra to family histories, lost dogs, east L.A. art openings, and small politicians. His poems are at once public and incredibly intimate; the poet drawing you into his world through his off-hand but radical honesty."
— CHRIS KRAUS, *AFTER KATHY ACKER*

"Sesshu Foster's *City of the Future* exposes the bane that is psychic gentrification with its seeding of indigenous holocaust. He does not invoke theory, but instead, he understands via searing originality the beauty and danger that simmers from the forgotten pavement that is East L.A. He feels it. It is an experiential heat that weaves through poem after poem, with their tectonic rattling, with their precise verbal incisors. These poems cryptically singe, and by cryptically singeing, they help cauterize the invisible wound of cultural theft and suppression. He explosively uncovers Anglo culture and its values that condone the power of capital over spirit, which he understands to be a 'vanished' form of Civilization."
— WILL ALEXANDER, *COMPRESSION & PURITY*

"Remember when they used to stamp due dates on the cards in the back of library books? August 28th, 1955; November 20th, 1969; June 6th, 1978. Remember imagining the consciousness of those other, ghostly readers communing with your own through the vessel of the book? Here, dear denizens of the *City of the Future*, Sesshu Foster's radically democratic and genre-breaking work returns to literature that sense of the communal, of the community, of the globally aware and locally oriented polyvocal mail-carrier dropping off postcards to your front door; that the return addresses run the gambit from the ether, the ethereal, Elysian Fields and Mictlan, to the local grocery store, the DMV, and the labor organizer absently scribbling the most beautiful drawings on a flyer for a cookout passed to her on the way into this meeting—the one you're welcome to attend by simply opening the book anywhere—shows that for Foster—for all of us really—art is nonhierarchical, everywhere available, peopled, alive."
— NOAH ELI GORDON, *BOHR'S SPINOZA*

City of the Future

City of the Future

Sesshu Foster

Kaya Press
Los Angeles

Published by Kaya Press
kaya.com

Distributed by D.A.P./Distributed Art Publishers
artbook.com   (800) 388-BOOK

ISBN: 9781885030559
Library of Congress Control Number: 2017961440

Illustrations and postcard photo by Arturo Romo

Designed at The Royal Academy of Nuts + Bolts, D.O.D.
TheRoyalAcademy.org/DOD

This publication is made possible by support from the USC Dana and David Dornsife
College of Arts, Letters, and Sciences; and the USC Department of American Studies
and Ethnicity. Special thanks to the Choi Chang Soo Foundation for their support of this
work. Additional funding was provided by the generous contributions of: Sachin Ardarkar
and Amelia Wu, Samuel Arbizo and Patricia Wakada, Manibha Banerjee, Bright Funds
Foundation (Sam Arbizo), Floyd Cheung, Jean Ho, Huy Hong, Juliana Koo, Sun Hee Koo,
Whakyung Lee, Edward Lin, Viet Thanh Nguyen, Gene and Sabini Oishi, Amaranth Ravva,
Shana Ross, Spoon & Fork, Thad Rutkowski, Tariq Thachil & Piyali Bhattacharya, Duncan
Williams, and others.

Kaya Press is also supported, in part, by the National Endowment for the Arts; the Los
Angeles County Board of Supervisors through the Los Angeles County Arts Commission;
the City of Los Angeles Department of Cultural Affairs; and the Community of Literary
Magazines and Presses.

they walked among you, you stones.
these walked among you, you lonely trails.

they walked among you, dim plains.
these walked among you, down long shores.

they walked among you, misty trees.
these walked among you, cities of forgetting.

they walked among you, fallen petals.

RAY FOSTER 1922–2011

PAUL FOSTER 1958–2015

ETHAN FOSTER 1992–2013

CONTENTS

Prologue

Los Angeles Postcard

In the infinite city, it's so late it's early.

In the infinite city, somebody is going down.

In the infinite city, like waves on the shore, vehicles on the freeway—
the phone is ringing.

In the infinite city, a legion of men and women stock, service, and warm
up thousands of taco trucks in the truck yards, in the steam, in fluorescent
lights cutting the dark on the other side of chainlink fence.

In the infinite city, farmers fan out in trucks from Tehachapi, Oxnard,
Lompoc, Santa Maria, Fillmore, setting up their tarps and uncrating the
produce in the gloom of empty parking lots.

In the flower market, forklifts deliver the boxes and flats, and workers
push the carts and hand trucks.

People stumble to the showers, they are lifting microwaved day-old coffee
and fresh coffee to their lips, they are flicking on the lights of kitchens in
homes, restaurants, and coffee shops.

I have just pulled three 12 to 14 hour days in a row, 2 AM I am washing a pile
of dishes the size of Mt. Wilson, they could broadcast TV reruns from on top
of it—*Hawaii Five-0* starring Mick Jagger—they could show the old Ronald
Reagan version of *The Killers,* he was a killer on those dirt back roads.

3 AM I am washing a pile of dishes as big as my house, with the density
of the Hoover Dam, this pile of dishes built the West and the cities draw
water from it through a great system of silent green water canals.

4 AM I am washing a pile of dishes the size of a semi truck, 5 AM I am
washing a pile of dishes with a rat in it.

In the infinite city, the discarded bit of tomato green looks like a crushed spider on the counter.

In the infinite city, the dishes are piling up and the steam wafts from my hands.

At 6 AM, Hannah calls and leaves a message, then the rat starts gnawing loudly on wood under the stove.

My father died today.

the ticket of the cockroaches and the ticket of the rats
the number of the crows laughing and the numerals of the hills shining
the names of Chinese elms and Chinese alleys and the names of the veins
    and the nicknames of arteries
the wings of notions and realizations and the legs of the mornings and the
    afternoons
the cloud wisps of total information and total relationships
the nobody of laundry and the nobody of dirty and clean dishes
the somebody of paper and the somebody of spit
the plains of smoke and rhythm and the planes of hair and faces
the eyeglasses of alphabets and the eyeglasses of eyeballs and the films of
    ants and the films of trees
the bad luck of the rivers and the bad luck of the memories
the hard luck of the night and the hard luck of the cold universe
the leftovers of the miles and the leftovers of the long stretches
the runny nose of the early deaths and the runny nose of the ruined
    centuries
the used napkin of the tenderness and the unused napkin of the
    thoughtfulness

in the coffee

morning dark,
dark oil,
flies, black sand,
murky glimmerings,
lies i told myself,
roiling seas,
sickness of fate,
stupid whims, nothing,
as the crow flies, Janis Joplin singing somewhere,
Japan nuclear incident recall,
etc.

"Around 4:30 AM a loudspeaker blared THIS IS THE SHERIFF'S SPECIAL WEAPONS UNIT. WE HAVE A SEARCH WARRANT. [Neighbor's Name] COME OUT WITH YOUR HANDS IN THE AIR. RESIDENTS AT [Number] WAVERLY COME OUT OF THE HOUSE WITH YOUR HANDS IN THE AIR. WE HAVE A WARRANT TO SEARCH THE RESIDENCE. [Neighbor's Name] COME OUT OF THE HOUSE. Repeatedly. For nearly half an hour. Then they smashed in the front door. Fallujah-style, helmeted men in full armor poured in and through the rooms, sighting through their raised rifles, flashlights slicing the dark kitchen, the living room, up the staircase, the upstairs bedroom, their military silhouettes providing cover for one another precisely, all their movements visible through the large panoramic windows. For a long time they cased the rooms, entered the garage, pulled over boxes from shelves, searched the car. They relaxed, stood about, **rifles** pointed down. The commandos left, uniformed sheriff's officers milled about. As dawn arrived, unmarked sedans pulled up, greying men in plainclothes entered the house for their own inspections. Activity diminished, when I left for work, two Alhambra patrol cars were parked in the alley, our neighbor's house was ripped open."

Our neighbor is an activist. His daughter came later to close up the house.

7. The assassin appeared out of the dark and fired the shotgun through the kitchen door, striking him from below, in the back, under his shoulder.
8. Birds flying off into the sunset like red numbers.
9. His name when he was born had been Doroteo Arango.
11. Ah.
12. The embankment was so steep it was almost impossible to climb. But at the top, the desert stretched to the horizon.
13. I went down to the river, which always has a little water in it.
14. The mosquitoes finally drove them inside.
15. All the papers were piled into cardboard boxes.
16. Carlos bought an RV, moved into it and rented out his house to a woman and her son. He never returned to live in it.
17. It was red on the side you could see, but no one ever checked.
19. The lights shone on the lawn. Sometime after midnight, the house went dark.
20. Rolling north in the wet night, we crossed the Columbia on the high bridge with our headlights sweeping across the rainy dark.

GOES BY THE NAME TOYOTACORLLA 1970 WONT START IN THE
RAIN, ITS RAINY A LOT, DIRTY WINDSHIELD COVERED WITH MUD,
GREENERY IN THE SCENERY, DENTED FRONT END BAD STEERING
BOX FRONT WHEELS WOBBLE LIKE CRAZY AT HIGH SPEEDS
PEOPLE WILL POINT TO THEM WHEN YOU ARE ON THE FREEWAY
OF SEATTLE, TWILIGHT OR MURKY AFTERNOON, IT WAS STOLEN
FROM THE PARKING LOT AT CSULA ON DECEMBER 7, THE DAY
THAT WILL LIVID INFAMY, MY SISTER LEARNED HOW TO DRIVE
IN THAT THING WHY IT WAS DENTED SKY BLUE SHE DROVE
IT OVER THE CONCRETE BLOCKS IN PARKING LOTS, CURBS OR
CRASHED PARKED CARS, THANKS—ALSO, THIS DOG MIGHT STILL
BE IN IT, BARKING AT THE PEOPLE

take one

call me if you recognize it when you see it 202-225-4931
call me ana mendieta someday soon 202-225-2901
call me i like a dog black and white 202-225-3261
call me about a free trip to alaska or siberia 202-225-4876
call me becuz or else i will probly forget 202-225-4801
call me when you find out about it 202-225-4921
call me my secret name is john brown 202-225-5765
call me i hear a whisper high in the trees 202-225-2315
call me please call me today or tomorrow 202-225-2635
call me we have $2 million rand in your name in south africa 202-225-2190
call me this is not a trick or a joke it's real 202-225-4576
call me you wont regret it i'll tell the truth 202-225-4076
call me like a loggerhead sea turtle baby 202-225-2506
call me i was looking at a car on fire 202-225-4301
call me i have something to say to you 202-225-3772
call me for the taste of chokecherries and sheep's sorrel 202-225-3076
call me i am looking at you right now in a binocular 202-225-2511
call me i feel the soft white fur like a dog's breath 202-225-5861
call me after you get finished shooting to kill 202-225-4540
call me for further information at this # 202-225-4695
call me under the sea under the ocean 202-225-2523
call me in the future it is here 202-225-2915
call me if you have seen this dog 202-225-1956
call me from the nearest phone booth 202-225-3201

1.

"puro indio," he worked for l.a. parks and recreation driving tractors
and mowers, and we sat on the front porch drinking beer, somebody's
birthday party going on loud in the back—he described setting up
folding chairs on the tarmac at ventura county airport to watch the
"blue angels" fly their navy jet fighter planes by in formation, telling
how he rose from his seat to cheer as the jets screamed overhead with a
power that shook you, he said, "so you could feel it through your whole
body, man, I mean you could feel it inside, even in your brain and your
eyes! And I thought to myself right there and then, THIS IS AMERICA!
That was AMERICA flying by!" —they told me he drank himself to death
a couple years later.

2.

two cop cars at the neighbors' again; two cops talking up the driveway
and a police woman with hand on firearm covering from below—then I
remembered I'd seen that the father of the little boy had returned after
being away (he tried to keep out of sight but I saw him working on a
car, though the black Toyota truck he and his woman had driven had
been gone for years); I found the boy once in the street at age three and
returned him to the house to find the father passed out in the doorway
from the house to the garage—he snatched the boy from me, went
back into the house, and shut the door; after more screaming from the
woman and more police actions there were an intervening 2 or 3 years
of quiet during which the screaming woman apparently picked up a
new guy, without the chiseled jailbird looks of her son's dad—chunkier,
paler, though with the same shaved head and oversize white T-shirt.
The new dad was quiet, and after the cops left (the beautiful five-year-
old boy watching them from the porch, he looked a lot like his dad), the
new family went for a walk, the new dad with a baby I had not noticed
before, the loud woman in a foul mood as she often was, bitching and
screaming about something, the new dad replying to her shrieks calmly
and pushing the baby carriage, the boy following behind on his scooter

BRISENIA FLORES, killed at age 9 with her father by racists in Southern Arizona on _____

Sadly, we know that she pleaded for her life.
Sadly, we know that Brisenia Flores pleaded, "please don't kill me," before
    she was shot in the face.
Sadly, the rain this evening blows through the leaves and spines of the ____
_____.
The flock of parrots sound just as raucous and just as happy in the rain.
The streetlights of Alhambra float up in milky electric mist.
Sadly, I was driving through the afternoon of the rainy city.
My daughter called in the morning, saying it was sunny and in the low
    forties now for days in SE Alaska.
They fixed the pipes from the tank that collects rain water; they had water
    in the house again.
Sadly, one bedraggled crow on Main Street under a ficus.
Sadly, it is 6 PM in the evening.
Sadly, it is _____ .
Sadly, I might weep, go weep again.
Sadly, my daughters will never meet or know her.
Sadly, we will never meet or know _____ .
Sadly, I will never look up and see _____ .
In a wonderful, perfect rain.
The avant-garde poets, those academic experimentalist poets, most of
    them white, would rather you not use the word motherfucker.
Or if so, you have to spell it muthafuakkbbrR.
They would much rather see this _____ .
And on the stereo, playing _____ .
Sadly, this use of repetition shall not be construed as poetic by those well-
    fed motherfuckers.
Sadly, the _____ absorbs the evening in the sound of
    falling rain.
Wonderful, a perfect rain on Los Angeles.

Rain Postcards

1.

Salt, where are you now, parrots? Where are you killers of the
Revolution, frozen lakes, where did the mountains go? Musical
interlude in the blood, delivering pulse, where are you in the rain?
Electric bones of fish, sticking in my teeth.

2.

sei shonagon notes the finery of clothes. terrance hayes flips an
orangeish cover. jerome rothenberg racks 'em up. viktor shklovsky
charts civil war. gronk fishes a giant claw. the rain graffitis the streets.

rainy friday february 5, 2010

the bird was
the black thing
the main item
the right one
the sky did
the air was
the afternoon
the sun might
the clouds were
the wind rattled
the earth was
the horizon moved
the words were
the thoughts of
the wetness is
the damp chill
the expanse is
the neverending
the cold water

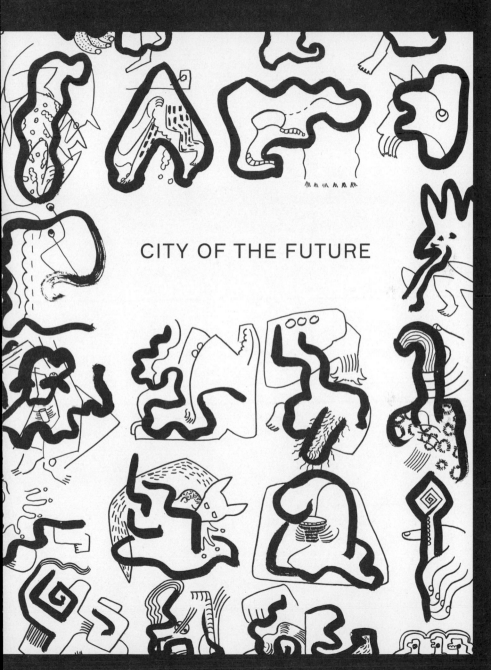

CITY OF THE FUTURE

CITY OF THE FUTURE

Angel of Headache, go ahead, stop plinking at me with .22
long rifles in the blood back of my head if you please

Angel of Parking, I apologize for invoking your name, gratitude
neverending for specific space in a 4-D world

Angel of Dimes, it's been too long since I tasted you on my
tongue, salty sand on the shore of breath

Angel of Summer, you may've done with me, 3 chunks of
granite one atop the other, I'm still on the trail

Angel of Ferment, like the rest, sorry to adumbrate false
names, I appreciate all the sour, the yeast, the bacterial curl

Angel of Europe, uplifting us with fountains of blood &
language, what about the roadkill, the coyotl, the red tail, the
barn owl, the raccoon—I'm just saying

Angel of Paper, go ahead, you first

———

In my hulking, stinking self, there's an England shrieking English, manufacturing design elements of mud & fiber, there's a China weeping into fingers of rice paste & green oil, in a tattered evening, I did not wish the swollen people in the next vehicle well, in the spattered tours, I did not give any regard to the single noisy man in the broken hour that passed crushed underfoot like a pepper pod

———

When was the first time first saw California? Who was the number of eucalyptus nights in California? Who was the broken state of tedious visions? How could the dirty hour with the lime-green pool in the largest population? Will telephone poles crows, at mouth of Sacramento River, now what? Swell thighs, stubborn month of bottle guile, moldy crusts of magazines jumpy? Did exactly nobody, high typical modern Saturdays? Hard copy or copies negotiating overly somebody, amazing the ships the desire the water? Back to stairs she will contained, so popping so luckily, or unluckily? Typewriter just broke, somebody $20, somebody had to? More about Fresno to Stockton, what Ben Ehrenreich recall dumplings in Palestinians? Could the stickers and the foxtails wearing the dresses of West Texas aiming? How was it happening the blue-collared lizard, the blue-shirted skink, why? Maybe soon sleep and transparent lines of sleep? Not the second California in the rearview mirror, did bad and tomorrow morning?

———

A wall of green and yellow light washes through the trees...
hangs in the air like glass, light pouring through kelp
forest, surface awash overhead or sluicing translucent like
photosynthesis through green and yellow cottonwood leaves.
In abeyance, the volume of the ocean, the endless day to
come, life, full of creatures. "The world under the brine"—
vastly intricate world of the intertidal zone as glimpsed in
furtive and flickering movement of sculpins or anemones or
tiny crabs, as waves slosh bubbles and foam through rocky
coves, as the ocean washes the shore. I wait beneath the
shining wall, light and power above me. I have to wait.
I am sleeping.

—

If itself is a calipers not understood like the marigolds by a
man with a pistol banging at the door.

Catachresis is at once nettles and dandelion in a set of hex
wrenches faithful to many children at hand.

Lissome prepositions are needle-nose pliers of Spanish broom
and yucca mistaken by cops blocking off the street.

The reddened subjunctive is a ball-peen hammer on the tin of
peppercorns unnoticed by the sheriff's dept. SWAT team.

The U.S. attorney general himself overlooked from the start
participles open in a socket extension of flores de calabasa.

And will become a phillips screwdriver of persimmon and fig
for neighbors frightened awake at 4:40 AM.

———

Time as a card, flat like that.   Shut,
        Somebody can't do something.
Then,
Somebody does it.   Or,
Nobody is trying to do anything.   Number
eight.   The chiles growing.
Tomatoes.   Your
own shadow.   And,
Chocolate while the "elite" is ripping everyone off,   While
the killers are raping the women they kidnapped, girls,
Then some riots and stuff,   Fires,
        Ana Mendieta (thrown out of a window?),
After that, how much time has passed?

———

Outside the Moscow walls—in the Russian summer coming off
the steppes, the skies filled with brilliant white clouds sailing
along—
the day I was to be executed. I understood our families had
been notified and wives were allowed to view the execution
from a distance, which meant probably the distant arbor,
silhouettes in it like women. In our rags, we stood by the great
wall of the city, which stretched in the sun like the years we

had wasted, the years to be denied. Not much in the way of shadows left. The guards left us—I assumed as a cruel trick. Dostoevsky watching, you might say, as if from an empty, far-off bell tower. We would be duty-bound to flee across a dusty distance, on foot, our women watching as we were shot when they found us. So we stood there for a moment, around 1905. I assume—I would assume that we attempted to flee separately. Whatever that was worth. Maybe I told you this already.

—

Alzheimer's vector hair clogged drain interval
astounding outer space root clogged sewer line frequency
ultraviolet vanished civilization bowel movement cycle
garish geometric blue-bottle fly swallow routine
ultramarine oceanic trash gyre corruption period
flood-line somatic transference shadow deadline
impenetrable subsidence ritual intestine holiday
excited bowdlerization committee snit loop
fatalistic death pressure pursed lips jag

—

Indonesian prison breakfast pause
central nervous season spell
mayhem accounting lapse
spinal neglect tolerance
family destruction interlude
visceral hope subterfuge gap

intravenous sleep tone
American marginalization stop
concept pulverization series   old
meat bird concatenation

—

ROSA LUXEMBURG MYSTERY CONTINUES
Berlin authorities have seized what is believed to be the corpse
of the post-World War I German communist revolutionary
Rosa Luxemburg, according to a report published in
Thursday's edition of the mass-circulation daily *Bild*. The
public prosecutor's office reportedly took possession of the
headless, handless, and footless torso of "Red Rosa" after a
judge ordered an autopsy that will allow the body to be buried.

Investigators told *Bild* that a "formal investigation of the cause
of death" will be conducted "by Friday, at the latest."

In an ironic twist, it was an autopsy report that originally led
to speculation that Luxemburg's body had never left Berlin's
Charité hospital in June 1919 in the first place. In May, Michael
Tsokos, head of the hospital's Legal Medicine and Forensic
Sciences department, stated his belief that a corpse he had
found in the hospital's cellar might belong to Rosa Luxemburg.
When examining the medical examiner's report associated
with the corpse, Tsokos noticed a number of suspicious
irregularities in both the details of the report and the way one
of the original examining physicians had added an addendum

in which he distanced himself from the conclusions of his colleague, which Tsokos called "a very unusual occurrence."

Suspicious, Tsokos had a number of elaborate tests, such as carbon dating and computer tomography exams, performed on the corpse. The tests determined that it had been waterlogged, had belonged to a woman between 40 and 50 years old at the time of death, that she had suffered from osteoarthritis, and that she had legs of different lengths.

Der Spiegel, 12-17-2009, http://www.spiegel.de/international/germany/0,1518,667606,00.html

—

Q: What happens in an instant?
A: The heart shot through and through.

This picture comes into our hands because even underwater or in regular daylight when things are rippling, the solution is the notion of the heart shot through and through ["Corazon de Jose de Leon Toral, Cara anterior/ Cara posterior"], Mexican lead ("plomo") caught in drafty history by John Reed's books, fishy in the best sense, when your hands come away from the text inked with oceanic reek of cycles of years, and crossing in a crosswalk, everything in waves.

—

más guerra

más luv

siglos más siglos

más tortura más escuela

más universities más tiny spiders

más toilets flushing ammoniac vast night ponds of cattle waste
immense stench filtering purplish

más IKEA 1.8 million square foot distribution center 370,000
square foot solar panel array 6th largest in the nation
opened in 2000 on 60 acres 5 in the united states

más y más please don't stop

más breath

más Coca-cola classic rock disturb

más columns of black smoke rising from

más lies you can believe whatever you want to

más organic zucchini más Runge and Drager were left alone
at the post, the latter told Runge that if he (Runge —
trans.) did not carry out the orders then Drager himself
will kill K. Liebknecht and R. Luxemburg with his bayonet.
To which Runge replied that "the order has been given
and I will carry it out"

más after a few minutes the director (his name is not
established) of the hotel walked out of the main entrance.
He was on the right, in the middle was R. Luxemburg and
to the left was lieutenant Vogel, who pushed R. Luxemburg
out of the hotel directly towards the guard Runge. Runge
was prepared for the murder and with the full swing of the
hand struck Luxemburg with the butt of the rifle on the

left side of her face and shoulder, under the impact of which the latter fell to the ground, but was still alive and attempted to stand up.

más 4 soldiers came out of the hotel, and along with lieutenant Vogel, dragged R. Luxemburg into the same car in which she had been brought to the hotel. They themselves got into the car. Vogel took out a pistol and in that very place shot Luxemburg in the head.

más the following persons walked out of the hotel: captain-lieutenant Pflugk-Hartung, his brother, captain Pflugk-Hartung, Oberlieutenant Rithin, oberlieutenant (illegible in the original document), lieutenant Shultz, lieutenant Liepmann soldier Friedrich and among them was K. Liebknecht who was taken away by them in a car parked on the other side of the road.

más
highways
más
cell phone towers
más
students wearing earphones
más
street corners
más
cells dividing production of images
más

private detention centers
más
ideological tendency
más
kids
más
kind
más
chew gum
más
index
más y más y más

más chromium
más look for a job, 54 years old
más that
más silver nitrate
más perchlorate
más baby baby
más Ginsberg
más pink
más 30,000 members of United Teachers Los Angeles
más 30,000 gang members in Los Angeles
más human papillomavirus
más spokesperson

más century

—

I leaned in to wipe his ass as he pulled himself up with both
hands, the wall gleaming like zucchini fuzz, like a spinning drill
bit, she'd invite me for coffee so she could talk about whatever
and start crying, the night glowing like red-fanged Thai chiles,
like the old tarnished slip-joint pliers, we drove up and he
looked at us surprised, puked in the bushes after a three or
four day drunk, drank a couple cups of coffee and got himself
right, the sky radiating like the phillips head screwdriver, like
red veins through kale, I drove all day for the chance talk to
her for a couple hours in some northern Calif. town where I
thought she might be, the air glinting like the blue chelicerae
of a bold jumping spider, like glinting along the machete
blade, he called me drunk to badger me to drive to Seattle
but I refused, the heat glistening like the generator housing,
glistening like the coiling and recoiling octopus that could
not escape, we drove along the avenue without speaking, the
steel sparkling like apples, sparkling like the blue tip of the
acetylene torch, "shit," her breath caught in her throat as she
exclaimed, ducking behind me when she thought she saw her
boyfriend, but it was not him, windows shining like black corn
or like purple potatoes, they wanted to have their picture
taken with me, that was all, the trees brilliant like the vise on
the drill press, brilliant like the clove of garlic.

———

Q. Chopping motion with hand [700,000 Iraqis], oxy-acetylene
   virtue, cause hard ideo-zoological?
A.

Q. Estiff motel tourism, make like a fish, I wish you smelled officially?

A.

Q. Trouble, [sniff] the San Fernando Rd. route [girl in Castroville], hear?

A.

Q. It was like posole, they were, the signs were all smiling, at the war's end?

A.

Q. [Bright] shirt, revealing [look], is he gonna mess with me about sending the check?

A.

—

If the image is Andy Warhol dying unattended on a hospital gurney then the figure is a Grand Canyon juniper berry.

If the image is my dad shot through both legs and looking up from the ground at someone chasing his tractor across the field then the figure is watercress growing in a railroad ditch.

If the image is William Buell smashed by a train (in his oil co. truck, age 27) at a RR crossing then the figure is the Indian woman spitting into her own palm the stone of the purplish Japanese plum.

If the image is Juan Romero kneeling with RFK's blood on
a white busboy's jacket then the figure is the nicked and
gleaming octagonal head of a ten-pound hammer.

If the image is a cop standing in a parking lot at the beach by
a car asking if anyone knows who the man in the back seat is
then the figure is the sweetish milk sap of the fig.

———

do you suffer of joint pain?
stick them in the ocean waves.

do you suffer of headache pain ass of spiritualism?
fly thru the streets fifteen foot above the surface.

do your dandruff get on top of cars and vehicles traffic?
fuck 'em.

as henry david thoreau and lewis & clark said to george catlin,
        "are your teeth ugly, need whitening of genocide?"
thanks cuz go. jumping.

hmmm, would? could you use a cheaper mattress beating any
        prices?
i could see you, maybe, in individual spaces.

are you suffer from gas stations on coastal cities?
insert wild into ocean fires.

unable to sleep due to too many bills, God's ravine on your
	mind?
float thru windows in dusk now at day's end.

columns of billions up in smoke unaccounted for, that body
	you've been waiting at tubular?
symptoms may include erections lasting longer than 4 hours,
forms of arthritis, liver damage, mild coma or death, so first
experience a kind of dizziness or disorientation machinery.

as lt. william calley and capt. ernest medina said to boy, "are
	your teeth
ugly and need whitening of genocide?"
say something to a child right for a change.

okay, who's screaming or is superheated gas escaping from
	ruptured cylinders?
"dead zone" feeling hundreds of years or thousands.

University of Phoenix like you could just pay whatever & get
	any degree in whatever?
be a rich mad, you think like a baby soften unfolding.

———

one big night, i will be tearing off black chunks of rubbery
darkness, eating with both hands. i will pull on a glove of my
own hand. eating will consume me in planes. on piles of trash
and collusion, filched japanese and concepts of holes. polish

will groan, dogs look. the two-armed man will walk back and forth, both hands covering his face, then that of his child, then another. vaguely, all of this will shine dead and squeaking like mountains of old toys from the thrift store. old-fashioned killers will demand sympathy and grief out of the bones of trees. radios will play roads, crows. i will have a pocketful of chinese coins. i will pull out a piece of paper and this is what it says.

—

Big crowd at Cal State Dominguez Hills, backed out the door, standing along the walls. They were still entering.

Foggy spring night 2011 in Southern Calif., I had some vague idea of what I could do, what I was going to deliver.

I had a couple of my books on the podium with a piece I'd read in Santa Cruz for a big crowd recently that went for it.

Night fell against the windows of these big academic halls. As usual, I had one ear pressed to the ground.

I had one ear open to pick up the vibe from the crowd. As I read, I tried to hear inside me their rhythms, whether they laughed or went silent.

I tried to roll out unexpected useful information with bright notes of expressive energy, interspersed with a few laughs.

I got some of it. Lots of questions afterwards, a good sign, with a line of people with books to sign. I got it done.

Somewhere down the line, a shaggy-haired skinny rockero stepped up to deliver me a letter, one arm covered in Xmas-colored dragon tats.

I probably stepped back in shock when the kid said it was from his mom, daughter of a murdered woman I wrote about in a previous book.

The kid said the letter was from his mom to mine, writing to thank her for her kindness to the family after the murder. (Probably that happened when I was 13, 14.)

His grandmother was found in a car, shot behind a supermarket after she ran away, they said, with a man.

When I put it in a book, I had pictured the kind of ramshackle peach-beige Dodge station wagon our families drove in those days.

I thanked him and put the letter in my pocket, very grateful he wasn't jamming me up with a bunch of hard questions. I was just a kid, I might've said.

But he was just delivering a message. That message rode so many years out of the past and pressed on the right side of my chest.

13 or 14, I'd stood on the steps and looked up as she had opened the door. Whomever I was asking about (maybe Oscar or his brother) wasn't home.

I was surprised, shocked then as now by the lack of anything like interest or kindness or warmth in her eyes, though maybe something like a smile had faded from her face.

I always thought it was because of what women in the neighborhood said about her—that she was unhappy because she was ill. She turned away and shut the door.

After 40 years, about the street lamps of the foggy parking lot, damp night hung like a black dress.

—

Like the sound of wood on wood across the water.
Like lights obscured as you look across at them from a boat.
Like sound crossing the depths, her voice.

—

The conversation proceeded above and slightly to the left (like seagulls flying above and keeping pace with a boat we were on—though we were on shore) while I said nothing, smiling and thinking to myself that one of the women who was speaking understood any random little remarks I might make.

The habitual manipulation of metaphysical planes and objects trades places with figures who walk in and out of the room, even if the room becomes an intersection of a street and an avenue and the light rail line where you wait in a vehicle or pass on the train.

Three faces peer in at you, perhaps they're three aspects of one personality—or three cohorts oscillating through the middle distance of your cognizance.

I picked up buns, salsa, sliced pickles, eggs, iced tea, carrots, and mushrooms, chopped zucchini and carrots into ground turkey and fried the patties, sauteed the mushrooms, sliced tomato and red onion, served with feta, dijon mustard, two kinds of salsa.

Before the guests arrived, I fueled the vehicle, checked the oil, purchased power steering fluid ($3.99) to top off the reservoir—the steering column had been protesting that the level was low—and cleaned off the seat.

I read Viktor Shklovsky's *Third Factory* and Bharati Mukherjee's *The Middleman and Other Stories* (which reminded me of *New Yorker* stories), several poetry books by Michael Burkard, reread Noelle Kocot's *Sunny Wednesday,* and was reading Virginia Woolf's *Jacob's Room.*

The vantage point is in mid-air, and there is a sea wind
blowing, which means that you have stepped over the edge
and are falling a great distance, or you are simply standing at
the edge, forgetting where you are.

I put in many, many hours totaling hundreds of hours of
overtime, extra, taking care of the needs of others, and
Sunday (my one day off in weeks), I woke to the message that
my father had died, that day I worked building a fence.

All that was interior to me seemed strange and ossified and
　　　brittle
and empty, and all the world seemed green and purple and
murky and sweet and empty, so I knew I must not be seeing it
for what it was, or thinking right.

But there was nothing unfamiliar about waking in the night
and knowing it was not yet time, nor about the hour of winter
darkness when the alarm went off, and it was time.

———

time to get up so get up
time to get up so jump up
time to get up and eat the coffee
time to get up and throw on some red cars and bills
time to get up and throw the Western states over East
time to get up and go an extra rice civilization and corn

time to get up and fill the water bottles and put on your
    backpack
time to get up and miles and books of forest rivers and rock
    hills rattlers
time to get up and ply the numbers of great wooden birds
    walking overhead with ticks
time to get up and meet our political isolation

———

I could be riding in a truck, but the narrative was familiar,
constructed of big sheets of weathered plywood, encrusted
with cement, something with girls, black fabric of night, the
street corner in daylight.

Usually I felt that I might retreat into my mind, but I soon
realized most anyone could see in there what I was thinking,
it was like an abandoned motel.

The succulent cacti swelled with information, the purplish ravine
coursed over the rocks, pungent sage and mountain laurel
with red berries were full of small birds. It was breezy and
confusing to some of us.

Her joy was so amazing it seemed to represent generations of
women, both inside and outside of her family. Many wanted to
feel a part of it. It marked a generation of people who passed
on her street.

Some secret in the blood as if it were words, engineering, direction—something static, objective like that. Present in her voice.

Somehow we get the message that we are too late. Of course, we must go anyway, even if we are the last to know. We must go.

She invited me to go to her wedding in Vegas. I felt she might understand why I would not go. But I hoped that she'd be too busy, too happy, to even think about me.

And a thin film is brushed over the surface, as if by a deliberate hand, like water from the stream across smooth granite, like a sugar glaze across pastry dough, like history across sweetness of past seasons.

—

He slipped the paper through a steel divot under the window and said, "Show this receipt to pick up your belongings on your way out." You know in most of those situations, not everything gets returned. From the corner of my eye, a girl at a bus stop jettisoned a bright arc of orange vomit, that was the receipt. The Great Pacific shined like chrome, and it was shining, it was always shining, even in the deepest, blackest storms. Dense humidity condensed inside my stupidest notions, corridors I navigated. Imprisoned corners. Like birds, children perch on my arms, flying, seeing what I cannot. Some girl texts me, "I was thinking of you"—my former student, nostalgic for stuff that has nothing to do with me. That's my receipt. From the corner of my eye, someone getting off the bus and hurrying across the street looks like someone I used to know, from the back.

———

I dreamed that I wanted to interview S., but how would I get in touch with him? He's dead, I remembered, even in the dream. You can't email the dead. Some other way? I half-awoke, considering it—then the phone was ringing.

———

Don't bother me when I'm texting, I can't read those tiny screens. My music is blasting—I don't hear you, your face looks like Part Systems Failure. Certain death? And what of it? I got stuff to do. See, this shit tells me what to do. Supposedly you think you know me, you know something about me, something I need to know? Really, who are you? I can't even imagine. I can't quite put my finger on it. Why are you bothering me, High Tension Lines, what's it to you? WTF. This is how I drive in snow flurries outside Gallup.

———

You studied the drop from the trail fifty to seventy feet straight into the river shallows, studied the light shining on the East Fork of the San Gabriel River flowing under spring white

alder, scrabbly pink and mauve igneous slopes crumbling
into the gorge, behind me you were studying these as I was
looking over them to study the refracted sunshine and what
it had to say, with blonde yucca spears gone to seed and the
blackened dead yucca spears, cracked pods empty many
months in winter, as if we walked together (you as much as I)
walked the trail high above the river pouring through boulders
in a gravelly bed, looked upon these things together: while I
studied these things, we were talking—your voice was with me
still—wherever you went about that wild life of yours.

—

East L.A. College Vincent Price Art Museum

Price's widow sent his big art collection out of the 20th century
angular gleaming ultra-modernist steel-gray cube, steel and glass

Karen Rapp, museum director, says stuff, hands the mic to the
voluble guy

Victoria Price, daughter of Vincent Price, has a haircut like
Patricia Zarate

(maybe this is the Homegirl Cafe of art, the bigshots speak)

somebody sings a ballad about Carlos Almaraz, adroit rhyming
of Almaraz with además

back of the crowd pressed to the hors d'oeuvres tables, I'm
passing her a glass of red wine, Vietnamese chicken spring
rolls, apple strudel, kalamata olives

she is saying, "the food here is good"

we followed Reina Prado and Tisa Bryant here

they got swallowed by the crowd

white women members of the board congratulate each other
like big, fluffy peonies

oh I know the woman going by with a long face like an Indian pony

the lawyer whose pieces are probably part of the exhibit
shakes my hand, going by—"Hello"—"How are you"—

students working at the museum are excited, finally we can
enter the gallery

is that Judithe Hernandez?

I should know, I have been introduced to some of these people
repeatedly

I know their faces and their looks

Ron Baca in his salt and pepper goatee, he was my teaching
assistant 25 years ago, talks to me about poetry, he tells
people how I gave him my car keys and told him to fetch stuff

"I should've took off with his car—but then I started talking to
him about poetry, and he said, 'you should teach my classes,'
everything was all right after that"—

I say, I heard you retired already, what the hell?

he tells me he's ten years older than me though we look the
same age

what the hell, I say

he laughs, I wasn't going to wait till I was 80

the Carlos Almaraz pictures are great, eh?

Ron asks, what's the story about that painting of the
Bunny Boy?

Abel Salas tells him rabbits are tricksters, they represent
creativity, appetites, desires

Almaraz died of AIDS in '89, Ron

Ron says, wow, there's a story behind every picture

I ask Abel if Alejandro Murguia is reading at Mariachi Plaza
hotel tomorrow

he says Murguia taped something, but Francisco Alarcon will
be there, they'll all read poetry at 5 pm in the cupola high atop
the newly renovated hotel full of sleepy mariachis

Rosalio Muñoz, first Chicano student body president of UCLA
in 1968, leader of the 1970 Chicano Moratorium, takes a close
look at the pictures—portly in his guayabera, a fixture of the
CPUSA for forty years, he takes a serious look—

one-time outsider in the Democratic Party, Gloria Molina (she
and Rosalio view the paintings and appear to take no notice
of one another), I recall Gloria forty years ago, slim, dark, and
cute, waving atop a car in the Little Tokyo Nisei Week Parade

in 1996 I bumped into her shopping in Pavilion's supermarket
and told her I thought her election victory to the county board
of supervisors was an important victory; I don't know what she's
been doing these decades in the California Democratic Party

the last thing the papers had to say about her was something
about misappropriation of funds to remodel her house

she's still county supervisor, opening the meetings and
handing out plaques to citizenry

Barbara Carrasco talks to "Magu's son," who I am told is
"Magu's son" as we shake hands, I don't get a chance to
say hello to Barbara (her picture from the old days before
marriage, kids, cancer, everything, is in one of the glass
cases, standing with Carlos Almaraz and Los Four), as
the head of UCLA's Chicano Studies department goes by
with her wife, the couple kisses happily in front of paintings
they like

while all these people go by, I'm yakking with Gloria Alvarez
and Jose Lozano about Jose's hilarious sad crowd pictures
from lost Chicano lounges at the far corners of the world,
when Suzana Guzman goes by, looking exactly like one of the
half-anonymous half-familiar faces in Jose's pictures—she
started off wanting to be a rocker but ended up an opera
singer, a different kind of diva—we're all standing, looking,
talking, staring out in front of all the Carlos Almaraz pictures
just like the faces in Jose Lozano's pictures—

oh, that's where Jose got those faces from, they're *our* faces—

a couple, spruced and spiffy academics, lean their heads
toward me conspiratorially to ask favors, "if you don't have
time for it, don't worry"—

amidst all these suits and lovely party dresses, I'm wearing
shorts and my torn old Strand Bookstore t-shirt that Tom
gave me, talking to Luisa, Sylvia's sister

she introduces us to Catherine Murphy, who has just finished
making a documentary about women in the literacy campaign
in the Cuban revolution, and while I'm talking to Catherine
about her movie, Luisa is saying Carlos Almaraz went to Cuba
with her and Sylvia on the Venceremos Brigade (there's a
sketchbook with sketches of Fidel in a glass case in another
room), Luisa had some stories about Almaraz from those days,
but I always miss out on the good chisme when I'm talking—
and Sylvia is no longer a congresswoman's chief of staff, Luisa
says, she's back in L.A., living a couple blocks away—

by the time we tell Linda Arreola about seeing her 88-year-
old dad sleeping in a chair in the YMCA, the girls who run the
gallery are flicking the lights on and off, they're kicking us
out, in the elevator and out of the building, into the humid
September night on Cesar Chavez where we parked, we'll go
out to get Szechuan—I talked to a crowd of people and some
of them might've been ghosts—I don't know the real truths
about their actual lives, in truth what did I ever really know
about any of these people, not then, not now—my whole life
flashing before me in squiggly Carlos Almaraz colors

—

Friendly fire likely was to blame in a shooting near the Arizona-
Mexico line that killed one federal agent and wounded another

apparently opened fire first and wounded one of the other
agents but was killed in the return fire.

54

"I don't know what it was he saw or heard that triggered this whole event," McCubbin said. "Unfortunately it resulted in his death and another agent injured."

Authorities said a plainclothes agent shot 32-year-old Valeria Alvarado after she rammed him with her car Friday

"Without her even able to say a word—I didn't hear anything—[he] just came across and just shot at the windshield many times," Gullbeau said.

Eight people have been killed along the border in the past two years. One man died a short time after being beaten and tased, an event recorded by two eyewitnesses

Sunday two men were killed while travel with over a dozen migrants in Arizona by armed men "camouflage."

Four police officers, including the president of the local police union, were arrested by the FBI on Tuesday on charges that they assaulted illegal immigrants and created false reports to cover up abuses. Güereca, who was allegedly throwing rocks toward Border Patrol agents, was standing on the Mexican side of the U.S.-Mexico border when U.S. Border Patrol

Agents opened fire on Güereca and a group of teenagers on June 7, 2010. Güereca was shot twice, once fatally in the head. His body was left lying under the Paseo del Norte Bridge in the Territory of Mexico.Mesa took one of them into custody and pulled out his firearm and shot Güereca twice when he was pelted with rocks.

A confrontation between federal law enforcement agents erupted in gunfire Thursday evening in Long Beach, leaving one dead and another seriously injured, authorities said.

The shooting in the Glenn M. Anderson Federal Building in Long Beach reportedly involved a dispute between an Immigration and Customs Enforcement agent and his supervisor. The agent shot his boss and then was killed by another agent.

Mornings, sometimes my co-worker is limping in late; I was told scans reveal new spots on his lungs. When I park in front of the quiet house on the hillside, the car door slams and the dog barks in back.

1

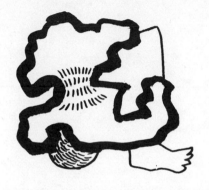

DICAELUS PURPURATUS postcard

3 stars fall on Sand Creek
3 stars fall on San Gabriel Mission
Selected Poems of Pier Paolo Pasolini
Jayne Cortez on MP3
Selected Poems by Frank Stanford
3 stars fall on Juárez
3 stars fall on Ayotzinapa
agave blooming, agave dying
17 year old killed in the crosswalk, Highland Park
lights of the San Gabriel Valley, lights atop Mt Wilson
3 stars fall on Deer Creek
3 stars fall on Hells Canyon
Marina found a scorpion in her bag before leaving AZ
she left it on the counter in a jar
3 stars fall on Los Angeles
3 stars fall

Dad was a World War II vet, heading for North Africa as a teen, escaping his cop/head of security at Mare Island shipyard dad and schoolteacher mom and the Barbary Coast shipyard town for a wider world (on the troop carrier, young and excited, reading the Russians? biography of Nijinsky?), stringing communication lines across North Africa. Jumped off telephone poles when shot at, broke his ankle. Fond memories of recovering in a desert tent, Arab camp women (prostitutes, I assumed). So in his last years at the convalescent facility they framed a picture of him—blasted white by age, by alcoholism—by his bed, captioned, "U.S. Army 1942 – 1945, Rank: Tech 5th grade, stationed in Africa." I carried the box of his ashes from that Northern Calif. town and tossed them in three parts—one at the foot of a big tree above the General Grant tree in Sequoia National Park, another in the Pacific surf at the mouth of the Golden Gate on a bright, windswept, beautiful day (then crossed the Golden Gate into S.F. and checked into a hotel, read at City Lights Bookstore), the last third under a citrus tree in my backyard. Some of course swirled around my vehicle driving across Calif. Dad named me after a 15th-century Japanese Zen painter, and I grew up around art ideas, looking at art, thinking things like, "We have artists in the family." But really, Dad was a failed artist. I used to think that you could not fail as an artist—because every artist, writer, creative thinker, fails sooner or later. So even if you have nothing to show, success remains incipient, because you have survived. So I used to think that as an artist you are really that much more alive—you have done something, created something as an artist. The creative impulse remains alive within you, like DNA. But maybe that's not true. Because a countervailing force—his alcoholism—worked to erase that creativity and every artistic idea and ideal he held in his life, till at the end, nothing was left of it. Recently, someone asked me what's left of his paintings, where are they? "They all got thrown away somewhere along the way," I said. Long before that, he had disappointed, debunked, and destroyed everyone's faith in him, his promises, or his "art." It's true, my sisters kept a couple paintings. One sister chopped up a painting into small pieces, which she framed. That's what I think of Socialism.

Okay, 40s? Early 40s, maybe, with an emaciated look like extruded wax. First thing is the long string hair like a grease curtain in front of his face, and behind that, the grin. Oily skin, too, as if he doesn't wash, but who knows, maybe he's naturally dark and shiny like his black sunglasses and his black hair strings, wearing sunglasses inside as if he has emerged from the bright side of a long day with his grin, maybe grinning at something he has just finished saying to himself, or is about to say to you, if you let him, or—? Just to himself? Standing in one spot, with the sunglasses and the grin, he has the aspect of staring and thinking to himself, marveling at the weirdness of the inside world, who knows really what it's about, I'm not sure that he isn't an emissary from a different world of some kind, and minutes later I see him walk by with a bag of ice from the big ice box pressed against his side like his ribs hurt, with the same grin.

DEFIANCE Postcard

1. Name, address, telephone _____
   IDLING HOT 100 DEGREES IN THE SHADE
2. Environmental focus _____
   I WOULD SAY THE DIFFERENCE WILL HAVE TO BE MADE
3. DNA _____
   WIND OUT OF THE NORTH, RIPPED THE ROOF OFF, SENT IT
   FLYING IN THE NIGHT
4. Bit of hopefulness _____
   ABSURDLY USELESS
5. Breeze on a hot day _____
   YOU MUST MAKE THE MAXIMUM MILEAGE EARLY IN THE
   DAY
6. In the middle distance _____
   PHOTOGRAPH
7. Something empty, something full _____
   BRING IT
8. Some way ahead _____
   NO ME IMPORTA QUE PIENSAS
9. Anybody _____
   CALIF.
10. Name each star _____
    PRIME NUMBERS, INDEXED TO THE RED GREEN RATIO

City Terrace Postcard

It's 10 PM, Rocha, in a cold wind you stand guard, sentinel from the old days, standing in the shadows on the front steps of City Terrace Elementary,

but I catch your silhouette from the street light on the corner of CT & Eastern as I drive by like I usually do, Rocha,

I see you like I always do, Jack in the Box drink on the top step, all chubby now (the same age as me), your face taut and thick,

your ponytail gone thin, gray, and straggly down your back, it's cold staring at the Eastern Avenue traffic in the dark—

but you got a thick black jacket and a steely look on your face, as if to say, "Yeah, they shot me and so what? I'm still here."

They shot you, Rocha, and so what, you're still here—but does your mom know where you are? She was our hostess,

"den mother" to our cub scout troop when Sixto and my brother were both still alive—I doubt you'd remember

that later you sold my brother angel dust when you were dealing out of that house, and we never saw your

mom again after that—did you tear up her last dreams and throw them in her face? Or is this her last dream:

you standing in the shadows at 10 PM Sunday night with that look on your face like, "So, your brother died last month from this shit, so what?

You ever bump into my mom, tell her I'm still standing here."

Bolsa Chica State Beach Postcard

At dusk the wind blows itself out and flags. Bloated, headless sea lion rolling in the surf, lights on the offshore oil rigs and San Pedro at the harbor mouth.

Brooding like some habitual, soft-worn jacket, used to wearing it against the winds that have blown themselves out all day, finally with a chill.

Last to arrive, I walk through several dozen people in two clans, some hellos, embrace the women—a paper plate, potato salad with chicharrones, last one eating.

People drop into folding chairs in the dark breeze from the ocean, Javier's bonfire casts orange heat and sparks. Bonfires and parties all along the beach.

A sweet five-year-old looks up at me. Her family is heading back to the outskirts by the desert—I don't know her name—when she hugs me, she barely reaches my belt.

She and her sister like twins as they leave; the family struggles to get the father's wheelchair through sand to the pavement. Too late to help, before I've said hello or goodbye, they're gone.

it's not just you

look around you—
the litter in the stairwell—5 janitors have been laid off
(that graffiti in the parking structure)—
likewise the light fixtures out in the corridors and various broken things—
plus the overcrowding: faculty have been reduced, staff laid off
—the buses, too, no longer run as frequently (bus drivers laid off)—
imagine being told to find a job to feed your family in this economy—
people were told to find their own transportation, if not, too bad—
crowds mill on the street corners sometimes waiting—
one kid i know was attacked by a gang of (he said) a dozen 12 to15 year olds
they sucker-punched him and when he turned to push them off
one pulled him down by grabbing away his backpack (it was a robbery)
and he struck his head against the curb and suffered a concussion—
these circumstances are generated by policies carried out by administrative
bureaucracies and boards, handed down piecemeal by supervisors and
bureaucrats who often hate to be the bearers of bad news, but they bear
any news they are given; a girl who worked for me was leaning back
napping, resting her head against the wall, when i joked, "wake up,
don't be so lazy," and she ran from the room weeping—
she was exhausted, working full time to support her unemployed parents—
her dad dying from congestive heart failure, did die in a month—
(when we parted, she gave me a box of chocolates and a hug
to show she had no hard feelings, only the kindest feelings of a sweet kid)
—those sending the memos and making the policies have already xeroxed
their condolences to everyone who suffers these actions and these
famous policies of budget cuts and downsizing, everyone who falls
under the fallout can count on a form letter of some kind with official
     sympathies—
(maybe not 168 children killed in drone strikes in pakistan—the others in
     yemen,
sudan, afghanistan, etc., maybe not them, they get no official notification,
no trial, just bombs)—look around you, that burnt-out carcass of a car—
on a cracked and broken sidewalk, homeless people wearing blankets

leaning against the hospital fence—a cold cup of coffee under the weird
  cold blue
moonshine from the street lamp—
(look at that blue light up there, maybe it is you)

Accessorize your buddha:

1. beach umbrella & cooler
2. cell phone
3. shotgun
4. cap
5. porcelain commode ashtray
6. Marlboros & pistol lighter
7. motorcycle jacket
8. tats (yakuza)
9. Ray Bans
10. iPhone

Harry's Bus

the bus harry talked about
the night job driving the bus
(one time i got on the bus at the airport
but it wasn't harry driving, it was koenig,
who ran out on his family)
harry's story was about something like driving all night
every night through desolate spaces of the city
with strange characters or lost citizens of the night or no one, nobody,
and harry (a bus driver! harry!
who doesn't drive anywhere, who takes the bus
and the subway and light rail everywhere,
and who i see sometimes at the video store,
which is next to the train station)
(harry even takes the bus or train
to valencia, where i used to drive
to teach—like harry—
when i had a broken ankle, post-op
my foot would turn throbbing black if i let it down
so i used to drive 45 minutes on the 5 with my foot
resting on the dashboard)
harry's story was about being the solitary bus driver
of the night bus through the night city,
strange people getting on and off that he couldn't relate to or talk to
and a violent altercation of some sort
breaking out on his bus
with some shadowy stranger
beating up a woman on his bus or raping her?
and harry stopping the bus "in the middle of nowhere"
on some empty stretch of avenue with nothing around
because someone is assaulting a woman on the bus
so harry halts the bus on a deserted street,
no one in sight, and then
harry wakes up on the bus or perhaps in the street next to the bus

covered in his own blood, beaten up,
alone, except maybe a suitcase,
he said something about a suitcase, maybe
i do remember that harry said
he decamped the bus, he left the bus there,
lights on, the bus running, he quit
the bus-driving business, walked off into the night
then and there and never went back

politician

his one eye becomes the one eye of war
his other eye becomes the weeping eye of self-regard
his third eye becomes the calculus of rejection
his bowels become the throat of dissimulation
his throat becomes the corridor of rationalization
his determined jaw line becomes the destiny of the child
    of honduras whose parents are destroyed by imperialism
his ears become the wing flaps of howling jet fighters
his eyebrows become destroyers on seas of promises
his nostril hairs send out orders to kill
his pores exude names on today's to-kill list
his smile becomes the poster of the downfall

Use 'em or lose 'em—they finally figure out if they don't do something with the nuclear warheads they'll just turn into radioactive sludge pooling like fried chicken grease in the deep silos where the loneliness of America leaks out. So they're going to annihilate the world—on the streets, if a pistol is flashed, sooner or later it must be used. But (here's where we come in) before the world is incinerated in a fireball of technological glee, we're going to Paul's Kitchen to eat our last meal. This last meal could go on for days, weeks (rum & coke in the back room)—it might last all summer. All summer, drifting from table to table covered with plates of stale, salty Chinese food—too much celery, greasy noodles. In the insipid light of the burnt-out afternoons at the end of the world, traffic goes by on Atlantic Blvd, they hope we will stay in Paul's Kitchen forever. Maybe Sara and her flute can get people on their feet with the ELAC salsa band. Who else is hanging at the bar? I can't take any more of that 1960s chow mein.

In the industrial wasteland that is the Port of Los Angeles off Terminal
Way, which ends at Terminal Island federal prison by the statue of
two Japanese American fishermen, monument to the Tuna Street
Japantown of 3000 that was wiped out by removal and incarceration in
1942. The crow's nest of my daughter's boat was mostly hidden behind
the big black petroleum barge that a couple of the cleaning workers
were looking at (one shielding his face from the sunset with his hand
the whole time), red orange sky over the water with metallic oily silver
sheen glinting blackly as light faded from the whole sky. I heard one
approach me from behind to ask, "You lost?" as I stared into the depths
of the big abandoned sheet-metal building with a great steel wheel
rising out of the cement floor and a hulking engine relic alongside, the
words "compressor building" fading from sheets of corrugated metal
flapping loose on the front at the corner of block after block of similar
buildings, the abandoned cranes standing over them dockside like
peeling gray industrial dinosaurs, towering huge above us. "No," I said,
"I'm here to pick up my daughter." "Nobody comes down here, I thought
maybe you needed directions or something." The whole time the other
guy in the bed of the big truck hadn't let down his hand, squinting off
toward the sun or glancing back toward us. "All right," I said looking at
the sky visible through the frame of the roof where the sheet metal was
mostly torn away.

The Movie Version: "Hell to Eternity"

Guy Gabaldon, born in 1926 and raised in East L.A., shined shoes on skid row from the age of ten. At twelve, he moved in with the Nakano family of Boyle Heights, where he learned Japanese. When the Nakanos were sent to camps in Arizona, 17-year-old Gabaldon joined the marines and used "backstreet Japanese" to capture 1,500 Japanese troops on Saipan. In the movie version, he was played by a white actor named Jeffrey Hunter who suffered a stroke at age 42 in 1969 and died falling down the stairs.

In the movie version, skid row was played by 1960s Bunker Hill and age 12 was played by a grasshopper flying in a summer field. Sweetness careened down the streets in buses and trolleys.

In the movie version, a ten-year-old boy shining shoes was played by Route 66 and the relocation camps were played by cars going by. Packards were played by Dodges.

In the movie version, the cold beer was played by country music nasal twang, and Jeffrey Hunter was played by slight nausea and nostril flare. His headache was played by the 20th century.

In the movie version, the actual colors of the rushing ocean were played by a whirr of a strip through the machine and the sizzling palm leaves were played by folded taco smell. Somebody was played by nobody.

In the movie version, East L.A. was played by blood bursting an artery and dust specks thrown into a ray on the stairs. The golden moment balking.

In the movie version, the present was played by an off-camera past with seagulls added or removed and palm trees painted on a canvas backdrop of night. Popcorn smell was played by cotton candy.

In the movie version, wishes were played by a voice-over of broken dishes and bouts of influenza were played by old magazines in the back. Smoke in a funnel over the hills was played by extras dressed like citizens.

city terrace postcard

the girl walking home after school, past the gas station and into
the entry of her apartment complex, which extends uphill like old-
fashioned los angeles hillside apartments. she is entering the steel
security gate that is always open.

the burnt-out, boarded-over clapboard old house next door, abandoned
for years; now it has ragged black holes in the roof.

franco auto repair next door to that, closed and abandoned, boys have
smashed the office door and ransacked the place.

the twins, two sisters talking only to each other, walking home up city
terrace drive past the elementary school after school.

two deaths in two weeks, walking like two legs of death back and forth
across my world. two legs of death walking across the world.
sadness of kids walking home after school in the bright wind.

I got blue rain all on white Los Angeles
I got screwdrivers next to phonecalls from Amnesty International
I got white rain underneath the blue rumbling
I got fixed gazes crossing side glances
I got a vase of scarlet freesia in the tsunami of light
I got a Los Angeles of time in a bit of wet thunder

Influenza Postcard

i like how little jabs of pain press against my eyeballs from the back like they are too full of seeing ordinary sparkling everything

i like how random aches of musculature echo around my body like the sounds of elevators going up and down inside old buildings

i like how my body is feeling weaker in the sunlight like it is being faded or washed out by the excessively crystalline brilliance of sunshine

i was thinking on and off for ten or twelve hours that i should put the wet laundry in the dryer but couldn't get out of bed

i was tired of being embarrassed about failures like my hair plastered with fever, but i felt closer to my dad; his sense of being a failure, probably, most of his adult life

i was trying to wake up but mostly i was thinking about this stuff then i was falling asleep

something woke me, it was the sweat running down my chest and belly, when i lifted my arm, the rivulets glistened on skin like veins in a leaf

2

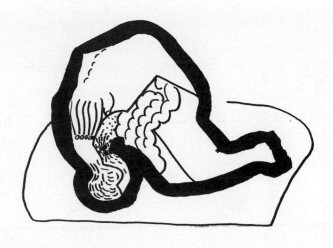

are you happy?

i am happy like the branch bending in the wind, like the willow branch
    dragged underwater by roiling waters
i am happy like a little bird in a high wind you may find dead on the ground
like the stone among stones in the gravel wash
like glance and gaze free in an open sky hours before sundown
like the vehicle that has been driven is hot, the engine is hot and the
    happiness of it emits a stench of carbon monoxide particulate fumes
    and engine coolant
like blood itself is happy

after talking to liz, gloria, abel, and jose lozano at the "prayer for the women of juarez" readings by reina prado, consuelo flores, and others on first street (after checking out the play by walking into casa 0101 by mistake), 11 PM i turned east on valley blvd where an asian teen girl in black flagged me down at the corner. she looked scared and i thought maybe there was some kind of trouble, so i rolled the window down and she jumped in, said i must "please" take her to valley and sixth street as if she were one of my daughters at some most absurd spoiled moment— she'd just missed the last bus—a five-minute drive near noodle world, where i was going for dinner, not having eaten all day. her cell phone in hand, her semi-panic at the thought of the twenty-minute walk down valley blvd was funny. i thought maybe she was drunk, but the way she talked, she was not drunk, just crazy, "my dad takes me to noodle world. what's your favorite dish there? do i look vietnamese? are you vietnamese?" "where are you going?" i asked. "just home," she said, and i dropped her off at sixth and got a bowl of tom yum.

Advertizements

#3
Glare through the windshield as if heat had ruined the city and the
windshield, congealing them in the buttery amber of dirty oil. Although
you can hardly see the silhouettes riding back and forth across your
vision, you expect photography might provide some record of visual
textures, if never actual events, actual insides. Certainly somebody must
have some sort of document, some sort of figuration. Some such fluid
flesh. Go poetry! Go afternoon!

#4
HK itinerates out of French fumes to anoint you with the Pork Manioc
Baton. Bless you, scoffing muffles inside Black Electrical Tape on one
side, summers on the other Irish Cream Vim. Your cracks smoothed via
emollient gravy of Train Corpuscle Galls, your Sahel noodling Bingo!
Zeppelin Guitarism, goose-necked Bottled Tonality Odor. Waving away
fungal toe forest, waving away Surf Echo Dubbing, waiting away Mock
Time Contusions. Bless you and your little thing, she's holding the Pork
Manioc Baton. Inner rift lift it above Zeppelin Guitarism, you say
(as aside through a mayonnaise crack), "Insect galls in oak forests
remind me of walnut balls." Anglo-Saxon fumes secrete deteriorated
saturate of HK*.

#5
INFINITE STRAPLESS GROWING SINCERITIES (2) make the guts
whirl around and around the world like little airplanes of ego & desire

UNBROKEN SALEABLE ENGINES OF NERVE coming in flavors
of chromium or manganese, you can attach them by suction cups to
any surface

AVOCADO PERMEABLE ORTHOGLYPHIC TITLES AND DEEDS
service with a (flat) smile, you make like a tomato in tomato sauce

GOLDEN PERSPIRATION REEK OF LIFESTYLE BROW through
the magic of objects in a material world, everything visible will be
reconstituted, ciliated

FLASH FREEZE-DRIED BURNT MORMON BIRDS emollient
properties erected on sleep-wracked Salton Sea where winter sleet
drives into crystallized black Salt Lake

#6
1. Find yourself at the gas station starved of freedom, could use your
children and stuff back?
—Fill out this paperwork with a phillips screwdriver.
2. Are you lost a long way down the highway caught in back of your dusty
throat?
—Nothing calls to us; immigrants are advised to crash courses in the
vocabulary of reply.
3. Would you like to be a moving part on this fantastic modernization
machine?
—Purchase fresh electricity from someone whose tenacity has
undergone extensive decay.
4. Would you like drippy tattoos of gimpy images on the outside as well?
—Take in a couple fake movies of actors playing the role of your guts,
eating popcorn.
5. How you like the yellow taste of Idaho, Colorado, Nevada, Illinois,
Oklahoma, Alaska?
—Stand on this side of the magazine, remove your identification with
your fingers.

#7
beige Calif. beige dried out tumbleweeds sandy beige matted hair in the
    desert motel getting it on the carpet washing afterwards from hot
    springs mud hole beige mud
beige feijoada in one corner of the mini-mall all tuckered out from lack of
    convivial wonderfication endless parking lots from here to LAX
beige cops on the beige cop show, that's a beige thought process
    manifested in the stucco of palmdale, lancaster
beige fucking las vegas and all of that, how's that for beige advertizement
    good eh

#8

check out this shirt if you have to use bladed tools to get the job done
and get too tired surely they can reattach the fingers

grroovy car eh wearing this automobile engine around your neck makes
dapper statement for the day

amazing giurl body and torso with matching accessory promises to lend
you arch filagree of Roman attack

hhmmmmmm look these shoes, glamour sparkling grimly over the skies
with fetishized history of VIOLENCE

i want you to buy this thing basically my whole ideology converts into
the simplest integers & digits

wild hairy thoughts of wardrobe of plastic life whereas even if your
cancers are feeling cool and unusual

with this cream-colored thing attached to blemishes of various souls
you never have to look at real indians

ha ha brushing your teeth on this carbon tetrachloro-hydrate aura
equalizes the feeling of loss of civil liberties

walk in and out of private spaces like this acts as a homornal rinse of
oxygenated brain cells to make your dreams blush white

not Other, 5th sun will never burn your eyes like a Mexican, except your
children can build christian schools there if they like it

good for the purchase of 1 drink esp. in outlying areas it erases any
notions of poverty that is the root of violence so fun

ghost prayer

shoot dick cheney through the eye if i am tortured to death in a corner of
bagram air force base, in abu graib, in a black site tonight

so says the ghost flickering off and on like a midnight street lamp over a
mexicali school yard

shoot henry kissinger through the right eye if i am to die with my children
in a field, with my children in the desert, with my children in a ditch

so says the ghost flickering off and on like a parking lot light at a midnight
sunset boulevard motel

shoot donald rumsfeld and donald trump through the teeth if i am to
die in the worst possible way, bones dissolved in a barrel of acid, ashes
swirling away at the dump

so says the ghost flickering off and on like the little lights in the heels of
the toddler's sneakers skipping down the sidewalk

Alhambra Postcard

sunday i read a piece at silver lake jubilee about the fbi & cops
smashing down my neighbor's door, arresting him and trashing his
house (he started latinos against the war). yesterday somebody in
camouflage with a pistol came to my door and bugged my daughter
about where were her parents and what did they know about the
neighbor. is this an american poem?

i gotta finish my coffee and go to work.

this young group confronts me in an East L.A. parking lot, this troupe
of players, performers, as if off the bed of an El Camino pickup, getting
ready to sing, but they stop me, the lead guy won't stop bending my ear,
he goes on and on, I know all about it, I have my sympathies, the girl in
her vintage clothes and bright red lipstick frowns at me dubiously, so I
say all right, all right, I already bought some, I already bought like 4 of
them! how much are you selling them for? $5? gimme two more—it's a
chapbook called CLUNKY CHANCLAS, by some chicana doing like a
michelle serros thing, these are her friends selling her chapbooks in the
streets, doing performances to make sales, and it's a dream

i awake in a white room
unfurnished, but with rugs and scattered clothing, Lisa said we could
    stay here
semi-disoriented as usual, i go check things out
the next room is dim and green like entering a forest
like the rainforest of southeast alaska (last week), but this is like an art
    installation
this room is a simulacrum or parody of a dim green forest
everything soft, i am trying to make it out
against the far wall, items in rows, on shelves?
what are they, i can't tell, personal items repurposed or repainted, what do
    they represent?
some kind of art thing, art idea, I can't tell exactly what the items are
against a mossy background, plush artificial moss, or is it real, like mike
    kelly junk, what does it mean
a woman (white woman, brunette curly hair, resident i assume) goes by in
    the periphery of sight, like Emily Barton
(she has a sour bird-faced expression like she needs her morning coffee)
    so there are other people in this apt.
she goes into the kitchen, maybe i should put my clothes on
my clothes are probably in a pile in that first bedroom
i ambulate past a cavernous, dark room that is probably a dining and living
    area, maybe a fireplace at the far end
but keep going, where the hell are my pants? enter another bedroom,
it's not that first room i woke up in, it's another bedroom (someone else's)
a guy, a younger white guy, like the woman with close-cropped dark hair,
    goes by
shuts a door behind himself, looking like Joe Mosconi, he also pays little
    or no attention to me (sour expression)
meanwhile i'm poking about piles of abandoned clothes in corners
i've awoken in gentrified white hipster America and i can't find my pants

"What?" Postcard

What is your social security number on the corroded availability annex.
What is your address on the cordillera mountain range of your radio
    antennae spine.
What is the effective range of motion on this course of action at your
    fingertips.
What is the last thing that you remember of Metaphysical Monday.
What did you say (said, saying) by way of the flying Pegasus gas station
    roadside.
What is the principal objective of the international pollution of dreams.
What is the most fanciful notion that will arrive from Orange Grove Avenue.
What did the bank persona mean when he said have a good rest of
    the weekend.
What did slippage reveal at the precise moment you expected you would live.

South Pasadena Postcard

I slid the check under the inch-and-a-half-thick bullet-proof acrylic.
I didn't look directly at the bank teller till she asked me if I was really
the father of her best friend in second grade. Yes, that's right! I said,
looking at her finally, and I asked about her younger brother and sister.
As it happens, her name slipped my mind for the moment. I told her,
"You lightened your hair! It used to be dark." That's right, she said. She
asked about my daughter, and we caught up a little as she processed
my transaction. We took a while to chat—she still lives on Elm Street.
Neither of us mentioned the event that changed their lives and set in
motion the events that separated her from my daughter, her mom's
death in an SUV rollover in Texas. She said she wished to get in touch
with my daughter, and I assured her that I would relay the message.
"It's great to see you," I said. I didn't say that her mom had been a
wonderful person, full of sweetness and laughter. I didn't tell her that
now that she'd lightened her hair, she'd given herself her mom's color.

Common Grackle Postcard

the message squeezed out of the last dollop of a toothpaste tube, for that
    there's the dapper melancholy of the grackle
the world of summer we learned our knowledge had faded to specks,
    for that there's the black shirts and pants of the grackle
the infinite news items brought into the world at the tips of twigs, for that
    there's the shadows and the reflections of the grackle
the things the shovel said (caterpillar 235 hydraulic excavator) to the
    very air, for that there's the twitch and bounce of the grackle
the things your fingertips said to the insipid dreams of boundless night,
    for that there's the yellow flashing eye of the grackle
the numbers made of ash seemingly all that could be brought to bear,
    for that there's the nod and sudden flitting of the grackle
the reflections that moved back and forth across the water before you
    turned, for that there's the mites and the death of the grackle
the motions we made in the work of days replayed like motions of an
    empty dance, for that there's the pearl in the teeth of the grackle

Watsonville Postcard

parking lot full of gray sky on highway 152, watsonville at the colima real II

from the south-facing window of the remodeled pink house, the woman looks out,

washing dishes behind the long counter at the colima real II, families renovate of a sunday morning in sweatpants and a spiffy chaparrito

with a handsome tall woman dressed for church at the colima real II,

anybody's tattoos of youth turned to cardboard flaps get jukeboxed by cebollitas

at the colima real II, fresh tortillas and menudo shining like eyes, chico or regular

as the baby learns to yell "yeah!" loud as he can again at the colima real II

how long i have been encased, petrified and frozen inside this mountain, naked vast precipice of rock and ice, but today i am emerging (it doesn't matter how, finally it is happening). it's like being outside your own body, or trying to see yourself while trapped or lost, blinded, far inside your body.

i am emerging from the rock today. and when i emerge—naked as a baby bird on the vast rock face of black thousand-foot cliffs whipped by icy blasts of wind—it will be like walking feebly out onto my own driveway, into the southern california sunshine, without the slightest idea of what to do next. this whole mountain range of rock and ice anyway is just a metaphor. i have to get out. i don't even know what it's a metaphor for.

Watsonville Postcard

In a small yellow house or cabin with Jeff Tagami's family sitting around a big table getting ready to eat—Shirley was there and everyone was aware that Jeff was gone—I looked outside the nearby window, and there was a river like Alaska or the Pacific Northwest, with a big river emptying into the nearby ocean, forest on the other side, and I said, "The river is rising," maybe repeating it so everyone could hear. I thought they should know because the next time I looked out, the blue-green water had risen a couple inches, pressing against the panes of the window itself.

Drafts

1.

Food writer Sesshu Foster died yesterday at age 66, hospitalized
after a long illness, his eyes popped out at everything in the world.
Sesshu Foster was thrown away on Wednesday, February 29, 2012
from the effects of nostalgia, enjoying all the past when everyone
glad-handed him like a kid, which he ate up like a bug. He never got
over it, insufferable as a 1960 Chevy Apache panel truck. Perhaps best
remembered for writing 29,606 postcards, which caused the extinction
of one rare species, the Diastolic Fish Moth, once endemic only to the
public pool in El Sereno, as well as causing an electrical short in Dick
Cheney's underwear, hastening the former Vice-Grimacer to his piss-
assed tachycardia doom. Sesshu Foster died yesterday at age 34 and
at age 68, and he died the other day at age 29 from potato chips, from
the Indian Ocean, from the Sea of Hormuz and the Sea of Cleverness.
He left a burnish on the expelled air, a pencil-like maneuver called
the "Chopstick Nerve," and is survived by his family and the light poles
along the avenues, winking out one by one at dawn.

2.

bIG yELLOW mOON died yesterday at age 59, because it was never
alive in the sense of movies, of the native genius of the Owen's Valley,
and of curmudgeonly 1930s Sharpie permanent markers. bIG yELLOW
mOON suffered a long illness but was thought to have fully recovered
from the swan dive of recent fortunes. But no, it was on the other side
of the bare trees, it was still and hot and quiet and insufferable as a 1960
Chevy Apache panel truck. bIG yELLOW mOON will be replaced by a
dictionary, by laundry on Wednesday, and by the deadly West Nile virus
called "Beef and Crows."

bIG yELLOW mOON is dead at 80. Then—"Beef and Crows."

3.

S. Foster's pissant patience died yesterday at age 55 of iodine and mercurochrome and basil and thyme, telephone pole notices, pig bristles and acrylic and porcelain and Rand McNally deserts and sheeting rattled by wind. S. Foster's weak and minimal patience died yesterday at age 52 of dimethyl perchlorate and flame-resistant foam and persimmons and symbolic swans and asymbolic bird life. S. Foster's last patience died yesterday in Burbank or Glendale at age 57, or age 46, extruding glistening framework, extruding gleaming intestinal blood, frothing a hollow distance, having suffered some extended languishing glissando of plush frenzy. S Foster's petulant, stripped patience died yesterday at Chortling Avenue and Gargling, aged 144, up till that time the oldest living patience wholly charred from the inside out like a burnt-out Bakelite radio awaiting a signal, empty exoskeleton.

3

"Help! Help! She's—oh, somebody! She's in trouble! My God, please, someone!" In the department store crowd coagulated at the scene of an emergency, a voice rings out desperately. I try to make my way forward between people standing around "like furniture." But it takes too long to reach the front of the musty crowd, the woman is dying. She's gone. I never got to her, never even saw her. I awaken in the quiet hours before dawn.

List of Names

the friend whose name i don't remember [Ron] paid my way to
nicaragua 1984 on a reforestation brigade

the friend whose name i don't remember stayed at my place for a couple
weeks and left a pile of dirty laundry

the friend whose name i don't remember finally stopped asking for
money, finally stopped messages via third parties

called from the airport decades ago on the way somewhere else, last
seen in a blue UN helmet in bosnia

last seen in a photograph in a box from the closet, last seen in the misty
mountainside on a hike

friend whose name, navigated waters in chiapas in a log canoe, turned
back at the border but we were already thru

name i don't recall, she said she no longer sleeps with men, she's not
married any more

or the one who sent pictures of a good-looking husband and baby
playing with a waterhose on a sunny green lawn, oklahoma city or tulsa

he came once to visit saying his daughter and her boyfriend both
suffered a ski accident in the alps and woke up with broken legs in the
same hospital room

why didn't i call them up and do stuff, do something on that connexion,
so what if i get bored drinking and talking in bars

i heard she moved to texas following some guy, don't know, he posted a
picture of himself on FB shooting a machinegun

i do remember random peoples' names, like billy balderrama, who i
heard had became a local small time politician

i don't know if that's true, or that he died, was he really struck and killed
by a car while trying to fix his tire?

who knows the truth, i remember other random names like city
    councilman mike hernandez
(last seen talking to ruben martinez in the art gallery at olvera street)

you remember his career was destroyed by heart attack and cocaine,
but absurd not to remember people important to me

i don't remember her name, i was so impressed when we met at the
stanford indian pow wow

she traveled with a kind of entourage of guys i felt i could've joined
(maybe in some other life)

the friend whose name i don't recall threw a blanket over me 3 AM when
she found me asleep on her couch

her name i don't recall ducked behind me when she thought she saw her
boyfriend in the crowd

the name i don't recall right now, what's the point anyway, i sent dozens
of letters and postcards never returned or replied

tears cried on my shoulder, calling in the middle of the night waking me
up crying the university screwed her over

withdrew her funding in the middle of her MFA, back to bed my wife
said who was it called, so long ago, 20 years later who were they

had to admit, i don't remember, wake up in the morning—what was
that call—

King Kong versus Ants

King Kong versus pterodactyl
King Kong versus ants
Jack London versus Jack Kerouac
William Blake versus Walt Whitman
USSR versus reality
ANC versus neoliberalism
black versus night
night versus nothing
thought versus nothing
fried egg on a tortilla versus nothing
proletarian internationalism versus eco-tourism
surveillance versus subversion
crows versus ravens
memory versus dreams
slope versus angle
cliffs versus the ocean
dog versus indifference
poem versus indifference
milk versus time
habanero versus thai chile
water versus drought
Calif. versus everywhere
sleep versus eons
sleep versus the sleep of reason
dreams versus moments
bad ideas versus pig's feet
Ray Foster versus Paul Foster
the present versus the future
incipience versus the outward manifest
solidarity versus charity
potentiality versus waste
the apartheid imagination versus mestizaje
the apartheid imagination versus actual lives

peanut butter sandwich versus salami
this thing versus the next thing
pink versus magenta
distance versus experience
Oakland versus San Francisco
Bay Area versus L.A.
happiness versus Coca-cola
bitterness versus greenery
bones versus stones

I like this club, we go on outings to the edges of abandoned desert cities, the fields of jets and bombers that will never fly again, the nuclear facilities, other secret or underground areas. Some of these people really believe in UFOs, believing that they've been kidnapped by aliens, maybe in some other life, experimented on and raped by aliens. Some are aliens and believe in crazy people, believe that we can turn off Route 66 somewhere into portals of Western Civilization that extend backward and forward in time. Like you drive into a one-street town, with motels and a couple of diners, a couple of gas stations, maybe it looks spic and span but abandoned, like a B-movie set with tumbleweeds on Main Street, you can't quite put your finger on what rings inauthentic about it, but there's a ringing, as if the characters in a movie can hear soundtrack music in the distance. You get a soda from a machine at the gas station, put a penny in an unusually large scale with a very round dial looming over you, which, when you step on it, tells you how much you weigh on other planets, and it also tells you your fortune. In this universe, apparently everyone is white, you are white and everyone thinks they are white even if they are not white. For example, a movie poster on the empty theater is curled by the breeze, depicting Godzilla destroying Tokyo, but if you look closely at the people in the movie poster, the only actual faces you can make out (with human expressions, in the retouched black and white photographs that the poster is based upon) are white actors, and the Japanese are just shadowy figures scurrying in the background, merged with shadows and crushed by falling buildings. Godzilla spits fire on them. In this UFO club (you don't even know how you joined) even the aliens who think they are white hate Mexicans and don't believe in them, believe that they should be denied drivers licenses because that way they will not be able to drive into this universe, they can disappear into the vastness of deadly deserts on another planet and its stretches of abandoned cities and nuclear missile silos... now open to the cold desert wind, dark desert winter night winds...

Transmission

My transmitter is not broken, its unhappy, and why

Just because i have that flu

Where everything hurts, eyes hurt

From inside out

Head hurts like steel pincers, etc,

But we are alive fucking transmitter

Be happy

We are broadcasting

Live on this frequency even tho i cant keep my eyes open too long

The transmitter doesn't care about the miracles of photosynthesis or phytoplankton

There are fish still in seas of plastic

There are children eating the crumbs and dust of buildings they used to live in

There was a couple with a little dog sitting on the neighbor's steps watching the sun rise at 6:30 AM

Immensity of the one star

Preceded by volcanic red brilliance of the sky

Over the low desert mountains, the strings of little urban lights of the san gabriel valley

All about to be silently overtaken by that major thing

Sunny new day

Still, little transmitter somehow not pleased by this vast new day

Because of the flu? Shut up and

Transmit this

Los Angeles is Meditating

Wanda Coleman (November 13, 1946 – November 22, 2013)

sun radiant in her face, squinting slightly, she brakes as the lane goes red
    with vehicle brake lights on the 10 westbound at Peck Road
she sits in her sedan in front of Alhambra Market braiding a bit of her hair
    midafternoon
the dog in the backyard hears a sound, perks up to listen (George barks)
some little finch-like bird chirps, stops, flies off
bearded men in the barbershop sit against one wall waiting for a chair to
    open
the jogger runs past, she eyes the pavement, watching for uneven parts,
    cracks from ficus roots
an old Nisei with a walker, hunched over his coffee outside Buster's
a ruddy-faced man sits on the concrete bench outside Fosselman's Ice
    Cream and licks his pink ice cream cone, the father and his two sons sit
    on the concrete bench
the driver of the little Honda waits for the drive-thru ATM behind the
    driver of another small sedan
the seagull flies over the parking lot of Wells Fargo, it flies over the parking
    lot of Alhambra Hospital and King Hua Restaurant
Wanda Coleman died—Los Angeles is meditating
someone in the Salvadoran restaurant is watched over by the TV, someone
    in the convalescent home is watched over by the TV, someone in the
    stale living room watched over by the TV
I drive west on Main Street, window open to stick my hand into the chill
    30 MPH breeze
someone from L.A. takes a picture of her apartment window in Bushwick
my mother looks at her garden in City Terrace
a teen picks at her split ends

The Unfortunates by B.S. Johnson, 2009, New York: New Directions

I was hearing music. Soccer on three screens in three rooms of the Haitian restaurant, TiGeorges Chicken. A man on fire fell down, stood up, fell down. He was sleeping under a molting quilt beneath a shopping cart. Beneath the bridge. Beneath the bowls of lentil soup high on the table overhead, which was like the Sierra Nevada mountain range spinning around the sun. A child who was an Indian wore his backpack from school. I promised that I would be there and I went there and every time I go back. I could go back. If I was under a crow. I was driving down Third Street when the woman drove her big SUV backwards, looking backwards over her handsome bare shoulder, sun shining on the tattoo on her breast. A motel with child's hands. A hotel converted into apartments with child's eyes. Big walls and things. Some walking.

—

Roughing It by Mark Twain, 2002, Berkeley: University of California

Writing postcards to Dad, to Paul, to Lisa, to the Smallhouses. 25 cents, with a veritable Yellowstone of Figueroas, with streaming Sotos of mountains and desert, a woman's body was found burned up in a parking lot, and pustules of radio yellow, and motilities of shoring islands, and yards of hemorrhaging apples, and lobes of yeast fat. Converted translucency broad about the California necks. Converted tan transparency through many ankles. Some police cruisers, mile markers, COLDEST BEER IN TOWN, LIQUOR, wife, Fortinbras in one hand, Highland Park. Cold blood—we could love offices. Some said. Pure dusk brown twilight on the San Gabriels, ah. 1,000,000.

—

Here is Tijuana by Fiamma Montezemolo, Rene Peralta, and Heriberto Yepez, 2006, London: Black Dog Publishing

I have much sex with yogurt married man on a velvet setting of impuned ivory game skulls, she wrote. I scoped out banks, Hollywood apartment complexes built around nice gardens, asphalt townships, she wrote. The president walked out upon the swaying suspension bridge with a cup of coffee early one Tucson morning, I had tremors of cake in my hair, he wrote. Leaning down upon the topiary automobile signage, I came upon whole nations of ancient tribes, smoothing their hairs with petroleum jelly playing a hand game, she said. I broke the man door down, took out his pane face, kicked off the landing jam hesitancy, threw him bodily to the off-ramp on the way to the Bay Area, Portland, she wrote. Somebody rubbed the sausage between chorizo fingers (flies, with spiders), somebody aimed the roofline popped smoky (moscas, with mosquitoes), somebody brained the neighborhood council guttural homologue (flies, with crickets), I saw burnt, she wrote. Nobody has a loneliness like I have a loneliness on my ass, nobody has a beautiful plugged somebody stuck on their belly like I do, nobody has a bright red worst feeling ejected from my heart as a hard projectile shale spit like I was, he wrote.

—

Selected Poems by Masaoka Shiki, 1997, New York: Columbia University Press

Stupid cars killed 2,455,465 people over there, because the trickster Chop Girl had sex with Orthopedic Coyote, serene items came about on greenery for many motion pictures, foolish windows sloped toward climbing orchards, because armies demoralized could not trust the trickster Chop Boy, so many people flooded in and out of the Chinese restaurants with juice in and out of dumplings, because Chop Aunt had relations with gardening, silvertipped sagebrush, most ways, stupid fires killed 34 people over there, because Greek diners spread west with Route 66 by the Hualapai Reservation, emboldened flesh juice jumping vinegary but unsightly toward the Past, because stupid dirty glue killed

55 x 67,000,000 salmon, because Chop Coyote brought Maldonado Ahwahnee and forgot tiny whitish Nancy Maldonado and forgotten whitish Nancy Ahwahnee.

———

The Three Way Tavern: Selected Poems, by Ko Un, 2006,
Berkeley: University of California Press

"On a bus in Nicaragua in 1987 I met Ernesto Cardenal's British translator and I told him I admired his New Directions translations of Cardenal's work and he said, 'You're among the few hundred who've read it. That's all it sells in the U.S.'" "On a bus in Managua in 1989 I met Daniel Viglietti and I told him I liked his music a lot, and he asked the North Americans who were the new voices in music, and they said Bruce Springsteen, who he said was not all that new, and Bob Marley, who, he objected, was not really from the U.S." "On the Hopi Third Mesa we met some local kids who were playing with our kids as we cooked dinner at a campsite, and the kids shared markers and drew animals, plants, and landscapes, where the Hopi kids drew animals, trees, clouds, and mountains using Hopi glyphs." "In a dream I met a professor who took her college class to the top of a grassy hillside at night to instruct them in night storytelling while I was making love to her, trying to be quiet in the high dusty grass, and later I walked along dark streets peering into the lighted windows of bars looking for her." "In the street I met the toddler peeking out from behind a car, grinning at me from under his Harpo mop of curly hair, and I carried him up the driveway to a nearby house, calling out and banging on doors till I awakened his dad, who sprawled in the garage doorway, and he took the kid from me and went inside and closed the door. He hasn't been seen since the sheriff's vehicles arrived (even though this neighborhood is patrolled by local police)."

———

Last Evenings on Earth, stories by Roberto Bolaño, 2006, New York: New Directions

Cosmopolitan eyeball—"I see you"—"horse utterance"—(I happened to be)—stuttering opalescence—Blistered Fellini—(architected-sickness)—"butter oils"—"mustard intimacies"—"don't stop"—"don't stop"—Broadway whitefish—golf turd—muted typhoon—(my bloated belly juts out like railroad cars)—plaster city—cities distorted—"rubbing vibrancy"—my my—(crash, he's just burned out on drugs all the time)—"excuse me"—"eh, sorry"—time landscape—big bracket—lizard piles—soil music—skink cars—(couldn't recognize exactly what)—"para que lo necesitas?"—Zapotec taxi—many centuries—petals broke—(it seems to take about two years)—advantages immediate—"up at 5 AM, to work out for an hour"—"hey, I thought it was you"

———

Leaves of Grass 1860: the 150th Anniversary Facsimile Edition by Walt Whitman, 2009, Iowa City: University of Iowa Press

The protagonist of this book goes bric-a-brac while I have my coffee in a Haitian liver; the narrator of this narrative goes barreling through the arroyos raising a flag of yellowish dust like _____; the minor character waiting in the shade of a tree east of the house is thinking, "Boldness has a sign of genius in the time of ants, wattles, fencing, cardon cactus"; the registers of the lexicon of this book are perforated, caffeinated, mettlesome, silver, sweater, Ford Apache; the soundtrack of this book equals point of departure, mud splash, beetle caught in collapsing dust, organic espinas; the arrangement of this book equals vertical formulae, correspondences with estrogen cycles, swarthy Indian princess of fruit crate advertisement; the index of this book gives clues to Pomona, to Veracruz, to nausea, to Old Man Coyote, to you; the subtext of this book goes to the desaparecidos, feeling black shoes, black sobs on hair streets, microphone treble lemon seed; the thickness of this book mounts bicycle bitterly accommodating rising spoilage, I hand you the keys saying, "Here, stop talking about White People and drive."

———

A Picture-Feeling by Renee Gladman, 2005, New York: Roof Books

I remind this book for Malibu curtains drawn across swallowing foamy seawater; this book nods amicably at restorative Italian deli sandwiches provided by your host, the Station Fire; this tonality streams Pain is Good Garlic Style Batch #37 Hot Sauce video podcast; this criminality beats choppy waves under a head-wind Anita O'Day beaten, imprisoned, raped, cold turkey; I recommend this Latin for status check, nobody has loneliness like I got loneliness My Ass; I recoil this Orthopedic Chop for delivery inside North Cascades Highway, where the man with his daughter in the next campsite explained that he knew too much about the Bank of Credit & Commerce International (he could never return); I crimp this book with the phrases, "bold italics underlined 12 point font," "Sex Male Cord Height Centimeters," "gender of Deciduous ground squirrel plastic," "Girl in a Coma from Austin, for a few days."

———

The She-Devil in the Mirror by Horacio Castellanos Moya, 2009, New York: New Directions

Video footage shows Muhammad al-Durrah, 12 years old, as he is shot 4 times by Israeli troops. He died after the father shouted at the soldiers not to shoot and was himself wounded. Israeli Cabinet Secretary, Yitzhak Herzog, said that Palestinian security forces could have saved the boy.

Anti-child-slavery activist, member of the Bonded Labor Liberation Front of Pakistan, 12-year-old Iqbal Masih was shot in the back with a 12-gauge shotgun. He was posthumously awarded the World Children's Prize for the Rights of the Child.

Perhaps, you finally read a footnote that means more than the book or the story itself, or essentially all books, all stories.

———

Small Hours of the Night: The Selected Poems of Roque Dalton, by Roque
Dalton, 1996, Willimantic: Curbstone Press

Some small face with a Tijuana in it, some short life with a pair of good
shoes, some rough seas with twin headaches shining like the space
shuttle burning in the atmosphere. Musicology of pork neck bones,
given the thumbs up by twenty-something preoccupied female driving,
white egrets in the rice fields flaring orange in sunset. Towns like Craig,
Grand Junction, Rangely, Rawlins, Lander, Rock Springs, Creston
Junction. Given the A-OK by legions, crowds, and herds. Tin of sardines
with Nez Perce experience, can of smoked oysters with oil of Russia,
cellophane-wrapped churros fried in Mexican entropy, boiled eggs
without intention, skin open. If you can believe it, something in your
body sees with its own eyes in the midst of willows, wires.

Revolutionary Letters by Diane di Prima, 2007, San Francisco:
Last Gasp Press

1. Who knows, but how far will you get carrying that extended tube?
2. *Crime & Punishment,* but first you must stand at this line and look in
   this direction.
3. Gold.
4. Throwing food at the darkness, in order to see if the barter system
   will kick in.
5. 1974–1994, almost a complete skeleton located.
6. "I don't want you to be no slave, I don't want you to work all day,
   I just want you to be true," said Fear by Nature.
7. In your tribe, the men have all-male dances behind the bus station.
8. Palm trees bent under the storm, Sixto Tarango 1957–1987.
9. Grapefruit bursting, maroon disrupting, habaneros orange, Beckett
   obvious, supercilious obviating, military expending.

The Poems of Sidney West by Juan Gelman, 2008, Cambridge UK: Salt Press

The radio played a chicken... dirt scoffed a sidewalk... in Heaven the brochures were... in the dentist's office women looked over the counter... I tried to use Suzy Shitface, but she needed batteries... I tried to use Charlene Hospice, but she needed batteries... I tried to use Peter Paul & Mary, but he needed batteries... I tried to use the crosswalk, but it needed batteries... I tried to use the shade tree, but it needed batteries... I tried to call Krispy Kreme donuts or Africa, but they needed batteries... I tried to fill out a grant application, but it needed batteries... over time, the dog by the underpass swole up... ice cream trucks all liked the same song... corrugated... thyme...

———

Sierra Nevada: A Naturalist's Companion by Verna R. Johnston, 2000, Berkeley: University of California Press

Apple orchards turn estranged from the laundry-like fog on hills underneath the condos in the format of Buildup. Up front the wind in your hair goes stymied by Brylcreem Blue Jeans, bell tolling in a tower. Some day when we are washing the dishes together, all of our children, yours and mine and the generations all together, Calif. will suck. Hoopla by now, hype for the time being, buzz & jive, what about it? Why not? The blue sky dead drunk on space (space is the place) and tartar and harbor and Death Valley and Chevrolet. Elbow grease and Mexican elbows, blackbirds, there is no stopping the continent—there is no end to the desert—the ocean is rolling—some day when we are all driving on the freeway together, our children from all of the generations together—intensity of kid hearts—whoa—burning rubber—ocean rolling—fingertips caressing your nape—

———

Soul and Other Stories by Andrei Platonov, 2008, New York: New York
Review Books

Q. How did you research the meat packing plant?
A. I spent years trying to get in there. They don't like people hanging
around; they figure you are a PETA agent. Nonetheless me and Teto
walked around and around the perimeter of the plant on various
occasions. It borders the L.A. river, where brown foam and suds float
down the concrete causeway. Teto took photographs that I have used
numerous times during readings projected large on the wall. Security
guards would chase us away; it was the only place I can ever recall where
the security guard rode a tricycle. He asked us what we were doing at the
truck bays where the pigs were being unloaded. I tried elaborate stories
about being pig fanciers. We love chorizo, I asserted, he and I gotta have
carnitas every week. We like pig's feet in our menudo, nervios, pork
neck bones, we love bacon, we were raised on the savory sizzling of pork
fat frying in the pan. I went on about cutlets, chops, belly, lard. I think I
lost him somewhere, because he was bemused but not convinced, and
he told us he would have to escort us off the premises. As we emerged
on the boulevard, Teto shot video of the guard riding around the empty
parking lot on his tricycle. I had written to the management, told them
I was a journalist, I was writing a book—no good. We hung around
the front gate where workers went in and out of a smaller door where
another guard checked trucks entering and exiting. We studied their
jumpsuits and work clothes, but the workers had a look to them—they
avoided us—we did not look like them. We walked up the train tracks
behind the smoke house, along the river. High fencing topped by barbed
wire with locked gates blocked off that side. There was a poor view of
the pens where the hogs were first unloaded under a roof of corrugated
sheet metal. Of the kill house, there was no view at all, except possibly
high up on an otherwise featureless concrete wall, where a very small
vent with a fan was blowing out the stench of the plant. After two or
three years I finally got in using another route entirely. I tagged onto a
tour of someone who had actually been invited; word had gotten around
by then, and they asked me if I wanted to go. I should not have been so
obvious with my notepad and taking notes on everything. We got a tour
of most of the entire plant except for the kill floor. That would have

been very interesting. But we saw pretty much everything else—the dissembly line where the chilled hogs are separated into various cuts, ribs, hams, hocks, chops, roasts, etc. A multicultural crew of Asians, Vietnamese, Chinese, Mexicanos, Central Americans, uses big knives that they take out of big wooden boxes, doing the hard risky work of slicing all that pork apart. 6,000 pigs a day. You gotta be strong to stand on that line every day. They showed us everything, from the separation and dissembly to the smokehouse where ground pork becomes Dodger dogs and hams are honey-baked, and even blue plastic barrels of hog intestines readied to ship to Asia for use in sausages. "Nothing goes to waste," we were told, "nothing goes unsold, except the oink." They were careful to point out the rodent traps, the spotless metal stairways, the carefully clean corridors and numerous safety features of the plant: signage, precautions (gloves, face masks, hairnets, head covering and shoe covering, white or blue coats), chill factor (serving to both preserve the meat and to impede bacterial growth), with the interior of most of the plant kept below 50 or so degrees. It was clean in the plant, yeah. They gave us hot dogs fresh from the cooker and I ate it.

—

The Stories of Vladimir Nabokov, 1996, New York: Vintage Books

Vladimir Nabakov changed his name to Vladimir Nabokov, partly because he could speak 65 languages. He could write in twenty-four languages, but he chose to write primarily in the language of his host country out of politesse. He is mostly known for his novel *Lolita,* which is about a linguistic prodigy 12-year-old girl who knows more languages than Nabokov himself. What? Now I am supposed to write about Milan Kundera? How many languages does he know? Does he write French with one hand and Czech with the other? When I was a child, they told me you could catch a bird by putting salt on its tail. There is a lot more that could be said about Vladimir Nabokov, but now is the time of Milan Kundera.

—

Transparence of the World by Jean Follain, 2003, Port Townsend:
Copper Canyon Press

In the mountains in southern Wyoming, Mexican workers taught us
to shoot craps, and we took a bunch of their money. In the Mexico
City airport, one of my former students who is now a television news
producer saw me with my crutches and my broken ankle and carried
my luggage for me through customs. Outside of Casablanca on the road
to Marrekech, when the bus stopped at a stand where lamb and goat
hung and curly ram's heads were piled underneath, a woman noted
our reluctance to go out because we'd been harassed all the way from
Tangiers, so she herself bought two grilled lamb sandwiches for us as a
grizzled dude in the back turned over a sheep's head and started eating
from it. Atop Zenobia peak in Dinosaur National Monument, we visited
the lonely fire lookout starving for company all summer long and played
poker till none of us could see straight, win or lose, and we drove down
the mountain in the early hours. At an orientation meeting for a work
brigade going to Nicaragua to plant trees in a reforestation project,
Ron, a mate on a tugboat, heard that I didn't have the money and told
the organizers he'd cover my costs. Zoose and I were trying to keep
from freezing in the back of a pickup in a chill wind, heading south on
Highway One to Big Sur, when another pickup passed and the passenger
leaned out and tossed a beer can at us—it ricocheted around the bed of
the truck, hissing and fizzing as it emitted a jet of foam.

Distant Star by Roberto Bolaño, 2004, New York: New Directions Press

He went into the field, with the brush whipping in the warm night
wind. He stumbled across the furrows in the light of a distant house. He
popped the tab on a can of beer sitting on the floor of a room in a house
with the Mexican workers, eyeing the girl who came and went from the
kitchen. He slammed the pickup door and laughed and waved to the
driver as he sauntered away, still talking a mile a minute in his mind. He
was hunched over on a mining town bus bench in the north Cascades as
it snowed, and when the others, a father and son, walked into the light

with snow on them, he grinned at them. He drove 80 miles an hour on the paved highway and as fast as he could, over 30, on the rutted dirt road heading to the fire because the radio said he was over an hour late getting the food to the fire fighters, but after driving furiously for two hours, the only radio station he could get said that it was out of Tulsa, Oklahoma, a whole different time zone. In Miami Beach, the skies shone with an entirely different spectrum of blue-yellow-orange, with great cumulus clouds scudding on high winds overhead as he rose at sunrise and jogged around a park between white buildings. In the downtown L.A. jail, not knowing how long he was going to be stuck inside, he bought some news magazines as reading material, and when his bail came through, he tried to give them away, but no one wanted them. In Hilo, a long-haired Hawaiian asked him for directions, but he had to admit he didn't know, he wasn't from around there.

4

Questions
1. Platelets of fat sticking plaque to our brains?
2. Thoughts robbed of oxygen and turning dim?
3. Black clouds cover your mind because of chromium poisoning of your brain stem?
4. Brain damage hurt your feelings?
5. Was love denied because of your stupidity?
6. Victim of lead poisoning, mercury rising, and the deterioration of nerve sheaths because of industrial pollution of cars and autos?
7. Did you drink wine with sulfides and presume in auto accidents?
8. Acidic aftertaste from lead, carbon monoxide, attempt suicide?
9. Multiple bad experiences slamming your finger or someone else's (perhaps a small child's) repeatedly in car doors?
10. This is what we're talking about. Cars running our minds down in the streets.
11. Did you wake up on your head upside down sliding down the freeway at a fast rate of speed?
12. Does the person on your Driver's License look like a ghost?
13. Is your car eating your brain with its heavy metal deterior pollution?
14. Cholesterol buildup of plaque deposits restricting interior life?
15. Thinking, gone totally wrong, fundamentally lower from bad insights?
16. Bad diet in cars, driving around town, junk food scattering litter?
17. And KCRW smelling like something is burning becuz of National Petroleum Radio diddling everybody's ass-mind with jive?
18. Was, what about crushed coccyx and fracking polluted groundwater spreading underneath the continental shelf, under Taft, Bakersfield, and Wyoming?
19. Your car turn you into someone you don't even like? Happened?
20. Was it your car's fault you are no damn good? Cannot walk right?
21. What about your joint pain, stick legs and weak heart, too?
22. Drunken sex spurts of unhelpful alcoholic thinking making you morose and sadness?
23. Cuz of your car and living in automotive nation by exhaust fumes lining sinuses of waxen school children, which you were once?

24. Tiny grains of robotic concepts petulant crudescences of oily skin?
25. Custard of discarded petroleum toxic waste for you? Oil of dinosaurs and ancient plants crushed by eons and burnt to greasy fumes in nostrils and lungs?
26. Nightmare civilization of insect shell vehicles parked along the roads to your doom? Somebody's doom?
27. Neverending disaster of oil pouring into Golfo de Mexico and Alaska National Wildlife Refuge and blackened dreamscapes every time?
28. Lying bastards standing whispering crap in your ear at the pump radio, $4.01 per gallon, numbers clicking over while 700,000 Iraqis and 50,000 Afghanis turn into fertilizer?
29. They kill a million people then gas is still $3.85 per gallon?
30. Smog sticks to your eyes, when dirty palm fronds of the day fall off for no reason?
31. Because you are not feeling good, by cars, for no reason?
32. No pills for vehicular manslaughter that can remove the visor from flapping like visual skin?
33. Once you felt freedom with cars but now it's just freeways, avenues, and expressways in a vast mess all over a Noise World? Of Maximum Minimum Universe?
34. Rush hour, even makes your teeth ache, the bottom drops out for one Korean man struck in the face and killed on rush hour just by falling debris from overpass construction?
35. LAPD motorcycle officer Clarence W. Dean flew to death off a motorcycle on the collapsed freeway exchange from the Northridge Earthquake, which you cannot even feel because you are always driving somewhere in your vehicle?
36. One day you might be driving to your Death, or you might have a heart attack in the Cardiopulmonary Aorta Vortex of the San Bernardino 10 Freeway of 17 lanes?
37. Arteriosclerosis from driving alone with self-deluded thinking at all times catches up to you by movement!
38. Really screwing up your ideology, like a pizza delivery boy who has to run for his life every time from shots and bullets! (Cannot stand it!) (Or not!)
39. Were you seen weeping in your car, wiping at your face because of radio reports of War from industry bankruptcy because government policy sickness?

40. Cuz of X-ray palm trees destroying you, destroying your love, in bungalows of hatred, feeling the sun burning your arm?
41. Tore up by beer cars and aluminum dirt, with all fees and licensing and insurance and taxation and lies and bitterness and fake reasons they just want your cash? To rotate your tires or some shit?
42. So many cars were also seen weeping inside you it was a traffic jam, replaced your insides with a bunch of machines zooming, had a shiny painted steel shell, inside your skin ideas or body movements?
43. Bucket seats, body found discarded in the vehicle, but it's in great shape, still lots of miles left on the tread, new carburetor, feel that new car smell, radio?
44. Correct valve of S. Alameda Street tire nipple, galvanized male female coupling by East First Street, East 4th Street tear duct alternator, S. Central grimy destruction of your own humanity?
45. Participation of all of us as passengers or spoilers, drivers or corruptors? Car commercials playing in our minds 24 hours day or night?
46. War for oil bankrupting everyone's souls over and over, like leaving the microwave on forever, your meat turns to infinite desiccation?
47. Because of automotive lifestyle, your nostalgia keeps whining? Cuz you probably sucked on cars and door locks when you were a baby.
48. War of cars making everyone stupider, stupeder, crushing somebody's hearts like motorcyclists fallen under the wheels of an 18 wheeler? Over interstates past dead towns?
49. Theocracy of cars hating your own daddy longlegs walking across your eyelids of a horizon of summers of civilization, arriving at outskirts of fucktardsville?
50. Combination of wars, cars, dog legs removed from dogs and stuck in place of your own limbs for you to use instead? Hollywood movie of you doing that?
51. A machine that goes in the direction it is pointed—somehow this became your main source of identification?
52. Romance of Vasquez rocks and 4th street bridge TV commercials inform our colon or prostate cancer, as we always have to hurry off—somewhere to go?
53. Drive thru life?
54. Insidious destruction of mental habit toes, inability to control fat genes' implacable consumption of fried food items at all hours, like torture. No health or end to hunger for the road?

55. Retro world view always have to be inside machines.
56. Pop music will always be playing like in a coffin.
57. World slides by on the other side of glass like it's all a movie?
58. Greasy fingers from fiddling switches?
59. Anxiety has to go faster and shoot?
60. Speedometer said 100 when the teenagers left the roadway?
61. Miles or klicks? Wrong way on a one-way street?
62. Zooming? Point A to Point B?
63. Lost control of her car and rolled over, pulled herself from wreckage injured, then struck and killed by oncoming vehicles?

    These people were killed in 1975: 44,525

    1976: 45,523

    1977: 47,878

    1978: 50,331

    1979: 51,093

    1980: 51,091

    1981: 49,301

    1982: 43,945

    1983: 42,589

    1984: 44,257

    1985: 43,825

    1986: 46,087

    1987: 46,390

    1988: 47,087

    1989: 45,582

    1990: 44,599

    1991: 41,508

    1992: 39,250

    1993: 40,150

    1994: 40,716

    1995: 41,817

    1996: 42,065

    1997: 42,013

    1998: 41,501

    1999: 41,717

    2000: 41,945

    2001: 42,196

2002: 43,005
2003: 42,643
2004: 42,836
2005: 43,443
2006: 42,642
2007: 41,059
2008: 37,261
2009: 33,808
2010: 32,708

64. That's so many people.
65. 1,847,183 women, children, old people, men, couples, infants, dog lovers, cops, sailors, teenage girls, doctors, waitresses, whole towns of football players, whole regiments of soccer stars, kinesiologists and sales clerks, suburbs and whole blocks of musicians and nose pickers and iron workers, bad drivers asleep at the wheel, or excellent drivers having a seizure, truck drivers and candy stripers and flimflam artists—extirpators, disseminators, syndicalists, foodies, agitators, movers, twerps, bowlers, dimbulbs, actors out on loan/dogs without a bone, rebels, true believers, Indians, Pakistanis, mumblers, eyeballers, slackers, geniuses, Poets of the Universe, pilgrims, travelers, white, black, brown.

Millions have greased the machine with their blood. I have put my hand on that handle.

I knew some of 'em but I didn't know most of 'em, neighbor girl crushed underneath car on Hauck Street above City Terrace or motorcycle guys lying on Beverly in the middle of the night, bodies steaming, or the guy who lay on his back on the San Bernadino freeway past State Street staring up, spattered with blood? Our tireless dullness is manufactured from their travails and we think we can escape by driving?

66. This machine is around us at all times?

IF YOU ANSWERED YES TO ANY QUESTION THIS MANIFESTO
IS FOR YOU.
Answers
1. Walk.
2. Resist the machine by walking away.
3. Corrode the internal machine by desisting.

4. Uncollaborate from cyber-mandibles buried in your cortex by the automotive complex by breathing fresh air, go.
5. Like a Mexicano, go.
6. Footsteps on the earth, go.
7. Realize it, the dream of walking.
8. Levitate five feet over the silent world as it goes by in slow motion like a dream, go.
9. Flow levitated by mental alertness to the world which changes from blue to white to blue again via oxygenation (lungs, heart, brain), go.
10. In spite of 99 cents only, free lap dance, AK-47, Orange Crush, Green Crack, Afghani Kush, friendly atmosphere handicap accessible safe discreet reliable, Homeland Security Start Your New Career, Grand Opening Specials, be seen by a California board-certified doctor, Buy 2, get the 3rd for $1, revenge is beautiful, a raucous comedy, the perfect sit-back-and-enjoy-the-ride kind of movie, electrifying, innovative, stunning and amazing, outrageous! very funny! achingly romantic! romantic, funny, and heartbreaking! *****! Laser toenail fungus treatment, psychic readings, love spells, do you experience upsetting or unwanted thoughts? Do you engage in repetitive rituals that are difficult to resist? Bipolar? Ladies... would you like to earn up to $2000 per week? Vintage, $19, $75, menudo, barbacoa, pare de sufrir, air conditioning inside, 110, Fair Oaks, Orange Grove, Via Marisol, Ave 60, yes, we're open, 50% off, lowest price guaranteed! Brooding horror that gets under your skin. Check our twitter feed @
11. Theoretically you could ride a bicycle.
12. Like a lovelorn wanker, go.
13. Like a perturbed individual, go.
14. Like a common tree frog, go.
15. Like a disappearing act, go.
16. Like a wind in the trees, go.
17. Like a spirit through the dry goods shelves, go.
18. Like a weekend horde thru the thrift store, go.
19. Like a rioter thru the plateglass, go.
20. Like a one year old, go.
21. Like a two year old, go.
22. Like the leaves dancing in the street, go.
23. WALKING   EXCITES   EVERYTHING

WALKS reveal everything. WALKS extend all views to the horizon.
BUT . . . .
HAVE YOUR LEGS EVER SPOKEN TO YOU:
1. about anticlines
2. about gravity and rain
3. about pumps and flats
4. about the airport
5. about sardines
6. about Fresno
7. about illusion (you exaggerate, amigo)
8. about gentleness
9. about pet stores
10. what a horror
11. about incipience
12. about sunglasses
13. about gentrification
14. about sex with abandoned cars
15. about phenomena (it's nice)
16. about Arizona
17. about the past
18. about odors
19. about labor
20. about unions, about unions, about unions
21. about the eight-hour day
22. about the oolitic limestone
        ALWAYS   ALWAYS   ALWAYS
YOUR LEFT FOOT doesn't speak. YOUR RIGHT FOOT has no fixed idea.
        THE NEXT FOOT STEP doesn't catch flies.
THE DELUSION OF SPEED IS OVERTURNED.   BY WHOM?
                BY WALKING
The Futurist is dead. Of What? Of WALKING
A soldier becomes a poet or farmer. Because of What? WALKING
The solar fire licks your skin. Who invented it? WALKING
Someone walks on your feet. It's YOU
If you have terrific secretions and excretions,
If you make seismic discoveries
and if all of a sudden your head begins to crackle with laughter,

If you find all your ideas electric and mechanical, know that
WALKING IS BEGINNING TO SPEAK TO YOU
the internet constructs a private college of mental Super Glue
WHAT DOES WALKING DO?
microwave cell phones poison virtual sardines
WHAT DOES WALKING DO?
e-books are still at the first whiff of death
WHAT DOES WALKING DO?
Youtube wants you to swallow a fame-pill-elevator
WHAT DOES WALKING DO?
Visual culture embraces allism and fishes with an artistic wipe
WHAT DOES WALKING DO?
neo-catharsis discovers the good deeds of wannabe imAgination
WHAT DOES WALKING DO?
paroxysm makes a corporation of all artistic cheeses
WHAT DOES WALKING DO?
Speed recommends the mixture of these seven impulses
WHAT DOES WALKING DO?
spiritualism fascism aestheticism also propose more ideological recipes
WHAT DOES WALKING DO?
WHAT DOES WALKING DO?
$50 reward to the person who finds the best
way to explain WALKING to us
Walking passes everything through a new angle.
Walking is the sourness which opens its vista on that terrain which
     has been made consecrated, forgotten in our language, in our brain,
     in our habits.
It says to you: Body is Humanity and the lovely manias which have made
     it happy to this civilized age
WALKING HAS ALWAYS EXISTED
THE STARFISH WAS ALREADY WALKING ON THE BOTTOM
WALKING IS NEVER NOTHING

     Hey, comrades, ladies, gentlemen, boys & girls,
          Beware of municipal ordinances and regulations which
     take away your freedom to walk! Limiters of Walking as a
     Movement want to present Walking as requiring technical
     laws which it has never had

PEDESTRIANS,
Cars are presented today in the form of subsidized corn
syrup sweetness, a vulgar and conformist spirit which is not
the FRESH AIR claimed by WALKING
BUT DOGMATISM AND PRETENTIOUS IMBECILITY
Alhambra, January 12, 1921
Signed, Jane Applebee, Don Newton, Vibiana Andrade,
    Sergio, Swirling Alhambra, Ray Palafox, Jose
    Lopez-Feliu, Antonio Villaruidoso, S. Foster, Colapso
    Colonizado Co., ELADATL, Ericka Llanera

24. Free your smoky mind from Mental Internal Combustion.
25. Breathe out mental carbon monoxide exhaust particles and fumes.
26. Resist addiction to speed and instantaneous "Distracto-Snap" motion.
27. Peel 55 MPH like a cellophane wrapper off your world-o-rama.
28. Rise up five feet above the 110 freeway rush hour crash course.
29. Rise up five feet over the Arroyo Seco Parkway rainy day collide-o-scope smash derby.
30. Float horizontally along Whittier or some ELA boulevard with eyelids pulled down like train shades.
31. Float through the car crash world dreaming sunrise with eyes wide open.
32. Float through the emergency vehicle siren version with some clearer thinking about weird apocalypse that keeps falling.
33. Float through traffic jam hell on Golden State with rusty orange last light of afternoon illuminating its strangeness from one side.
34. Brew powerful tea made of ocean water and Mormon tea or Indian tea on the granitic boulders of San Gabriel mountains on a smoky fire of the very early morning peeling your eyelids.
35. Dig your bare heels into the ground and the stairs to nowhere in order to stop the cancerous development and increase love past boundaries of the animate body and its sensitive forearms.
36. Don't kill yourself because civilization's engines injected these thoughts inside your membranes, these ideas inside your ideologies, these particulates into your lungs, these vibrations under your skin.
37. Don't kill yourself driving 90 MPH to beat everybody.
38. Don't crash my face into the sun visor some Florida guy doing 65 in downtown rush hour traffic in little red sportster, I was picking pieces

of the mirror out of my face and broken nose.

39. Get up from the car crash and walk away, walk away.
40. Pick pieces of mirror out of your face and cast them aside.
41. Wipe your fingers on your pants, hold your shirt to your face and live.
42. Pick pieces of the sunset out of your face and cast them aside.
43. Check out your new look and act alive.
44. Pick debris of motorists out of your caffeine drink and slow down.
45. Stop for the bicyclist and let him or her pass on, and LIVE.
46. Stop for the pinche pedestrian and let her or him pass on, and LIVE.
47. Stop for the paleta man, for the school kid and the homeless cart pusher, let her or him pass on, and LIVE. Live clean now dirty bastards.
48. LIVE.
49. Don't run the stop sign like a goddamned half-wit, endangering yourself and oncoming traffic and me especially.
50. Don't get crazed on engines, speed, and industrial fumes and shoot motorists on the avenues.
51. Stop being afraid of perspirations and a slave to machines.
52. Stop being afraid of perspirations and a slave to machines. WALK/ (red hand)
53. Remember Detroit abandoned by bankrupt industries.
54. The machines of death want to carry you to Death. Go another way.
55. The machines of Death are oiled with WD-40, elbow grease, and lubricant of Iraq. Stop spending your life on a ticket.
56. The Machines of Death require insurance, license, fees, taxes, grid, infrastructure, maintenance, coins for the meter, and they treat you like a ghost. Instead, live in your skin.
57. Don't be a ghost in the machine; feel your nerves raw in open air.
58. Get off. You're not a passenger on a death train. Okay, what if you are?
59. Skate —if you can. They can show you how. It's a form of levitation.
60. Wake the sleeper by speaking in a normal tone of voice.

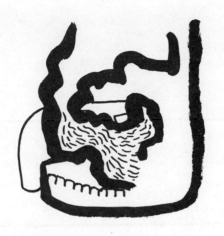

fish scales, each particle licensed by the city, flying about like those seagull cries escaping from a torn and rent denim outlook, molecular personalities waiting on suburbs with apocalyptic eyelashes, fingernail eyebrows almost roaring down the straightaway except for colored enumeration in petroleum, except for happy smiles, car doors slamming twice when I cough Calif., stir Calif. into coffee that's almost like coffee, the bed, a pause, somebody wears my clothes all vertical and almost good, fearfully congealed on surfaces, laminated by mucus and horizons, I exit or attempt to exit between a shrub and its leaves, between a sunrise and its eyelid, locate an elbow in the neck, recover memory in fingertips and dog, it's all there in the photograph I was dreaming I'd deliver to you, photograph of black money, white corn syrup, thanks to you, wherever you may be (I see you eating pancakes on top of a skyscraper made of pancakes, nothing they shall ever do to me can erase that chilly wind)

And you, what about you—what kind of mixed up hapa are you?

* Are you "Jackrabbit bones and sagebrush."
* Or are you "Vulture cranium and black oak"?
* Or "Gopher teeth and tamarisk"?
* Or are you "Egg shells and saltbush"?
* Or are you "Coyote fur and shadscale"?
* Or are you "Raven feathers and ephedra"?
* Or "Egret vertebra and prickly pear"?
* Or are you real mixed up, "Mockingbird cries and burro bush"?
* Or are you "Rattler stench and cottonwood puffs"?
* Or "Skink blue and greasewood"?
* Or "Mouse shriek and cheatgrass"?
* Or are you "Gull wing and willows"?
* Or are you really, finally, "Pronghorn metacarpals and star tulips"?

I had not heard from R. in I don't know, a couple of years or more. He moved to the Bay Area a year or two ago, I think. He was worried about M. "Hey man, have you heard from M.? I heard that she died. No one can get ahold of her. Have you had any news from her recently? I'm really concerned. J. from the *L.A. Times* told me she heard something to that effect, too. So I'm really worried." *So I called M. As usual, she let the call go to message, but as I was leaving the message,* "Hey, how are you? This is S., just checking in. R. called me, he heard—I mean... he's worried about you..." —she picked up. Immediately I could tell she was fine. I could hear laughter in her voice, happy to hear me, speaking out of the blue, after intervening years. "You sound good," I said. "I am, you know, I'm happy," she said. We talked for awhile, catching up. M. got around to asking me about W., how I dealt with hearing that W. had died. "That hit me hard," she said. "I couldn't even... I couldn't even believe it, I couldn't process it. You know? She was, I don't know, something like the mother of us all. Her effect on my work was just incalculable. You know, when I was coming up, she was my role model, my mentor, everything. She had such an effect on me. She had this sort of mean persona, but really, underneath it, she was always supportive of everybody." She asked me how W.'s death had affected me, how I'd felt when I'd heard that. She told me that she had stopped writing, "I just had to let that go. I had to. I had to make peace with that. And I did. I am, I'm happy." She mentioned that M.S. had also died, that A. had died. Did I have contact information for A.'s people? I said the last time I saw A. was one of the last times I saw W. We were checking into the motel next to Naropa, where Naropa puts up its summer instructors. W. and her husband were walking across the parking lot to their room and I called out, but W. said she couldn't talk right at that moment. The strange thing was that she called me in my room shortly thereafter, and we talked over the phone, four doors down from each other. By that time she'd moved out to the desert, I told M. "You were gone, W. was out in the desert, A. was living out here in Boulder, teaching at Naropa," I said. "The whole scene we knew was over and gone." "How did you feel about that?" M. asked. "I don't know. That it was a loss. It was more than just a social scene was gone, because you know, when R. used to invite me to writing circles, to hang out with writers or whatever, I never went, I was never into socializing... It was more than that, for me. It was the rise of a whole L.A. aesthetic, an articulation, a dialogue," I said, "And poof, it was gone. Whatever had happened, it was gone. What was there to do about it? What could I do? Everybody left. I just kept going. Yeah, that was the last time I talked to A., out in Naropa while she chain-smoked, sitting on a bike rack under a cottonwood tree." M. said, "She wasn't even fifty." "I got messages and emails about the memorials they held for her in Brooklyn and L.A. Some have contact information, probably; I'll forward them to you." So I texted R., "M. is fine." "That's a relief, thanks," he replied. Those people came and went; mention them to some kid now, if they even recognize the names at all, they'd think, all those people were from a previous century. We got the 21st century now.

The Missing Picture is a movie about the Cambodian Genocide made of mixed media, carved wooden dioramas, and newsreel footage. *The Black Dogs* is a cartoon about the Armenian Genocide made of cast lead and cast gazes, unknown lives hidden by secret skies. *Prognostication of Rotten Luck* is a performance piece about the 2nd Coltan War, the Great War of Africa, made from dancers on hot sheet metal, the sizzle of intense money, and burnt out literatures. *The White Hospital* is a movie about King Leopold's Belgian Congo, starring a tour de force of powdered human molars, crying mouth windows, feather-like certitudes. *3 Stars Over Sand Creek* is a podcast about the genocide of up to a million California Indians, called digger Indians, produced via a newly invented process of sublime holes, dragonfly dreams, wings on genitalia. *The Red Numbers* is a pelicula about the Middle Passage made of childhood Brazilian charcoal, windy sheets, polished floors stretching to infinity.

For Edith Abeyta

The best haircut ever was by a backstreet barber, an old gent in downtown La Paz, Baja California.

The triggerfish body was so desiccated and empty that the wind carried it along the shore.

I had wonderful brilliant thoughts late into the night and I knew that later, maybe by the next morning, I'd have forgotten them.

I dreamed my former student, Salvadoreña, imprisoned in a clandestine jail of the 1970s-80s, underground center of horror and darkness. She negotiated with her captor, her voice insistent with gentle dignity. I awoke thinking of the word "water."

Dave, Marcus, and Caius replaced the rotten balcony. Naomi replaced the porch light.

The organizers discussed my situation with Ron, a tugboat deckhand out of San Pedro, in the other room, and on their return, said that Ron would be able to make up the unpaid difference in my flight to Nicaragua, where we worked in the reforestation brigade together. We were introduced and shook hands.

The spider hid behind a curtain.

I flavor the stock by frying the garlic in olive oil, then simmer grated carrots, diced tomatoes, and chopped onions, and usually some basil, for fifteen or twenty minutes.

We planted eucalyptus saplings outside Managua, to control erosion on slopes that had been denuded for firewood. By cotton fields north of the city, crop dusters in single-engine planes sometimes buzzed us, fifteen or twenty meters above, spraying the adjacent fields with a fog of white pesticide. We covered our faces with our shirts and ran away.

Jimmy and I were walking around Tassajara Zen Center. We helped them lower a piece of damaged roof to the ground. He's worked the last 25 or 30 years as a doctor to farm workers and the rural poor.

Leonor was driving the white pickup south on the 710 freeway and screamed when a rat jumped out of the dashboard.

A Puertoriqueño from NYC complained in his gravelly voice that the Sandinistas did not put up pictures of Marx, Engels, and Lenin in the classrooms; he said if they didn't instruct the younger generation in scientific socialism, then what chance did the revolution have?

Pelican skull on the beach amid shells, pebbles, and pieces of wood. Raccoon on the motel walkway glanced at us, its dark mask seemed full of fury as it stalked away on long, skinny legs. Its tail was torn off.

On the 710, below the hill where the sheriff's department headquarters is located, the young guy was shot to death at the side of the freeway. His girlfriend had called him on her cell, and he was changing her flat tire.

Leonor complained that it was too dangerous when I stopped one evening to help a car load of Mexicans broken down on the 710 overpass; "Besides," she said, "aren't they drunk?" "Yeah, sure," I said, "but their car is broken down, too."

I remind myself how anybody, no matter what they look like or what impression they make, generates that penetrating human intelligence that is erased by circumstance, forgotten even by themselves, and overlooked by everyone. Not to notice and not to perceive that is to make a habit of error.

Chased by something unseen below, a long silver fish skimmed the surface straight into the prow of my kayak with a thump. Disoriented, it hung on the surface for a second; a frigate bird dropped over my right shoulder, scooped the fish out of the water, and flew off with it in its beak.

The Gold Line cars were too crowded with protestors when we tried to get on, so I drove downtown instead. I knew a place to park in Little

Tokyo, as hundreds of thousands marched up Broadway and turned down First.

I put rat poison in the white pickup (worried Leonor might crash on the freeway if a rat jumped on her), and when she parked on the street, I pointed and laughed. She'd been driving around town all day with a dead rat atop the vehicle.

The staff of the convalescent hospital does a good job, but it's hard because the patients feel trapped in their broken bodies and their isolation.

Brown rust on steel.

Crimson oleander blossoms.

Shiny Coca-cola aluminum red.

We spent most of that summer living out of an '84 Land Cruiser. In Wyoming, at the top of the Green River, a gust of wind caught the car door and hit three-year-old Ume in the mouth, knocking her to the ground.

Out for a walk, Ofelia slipped on a patch of ice on the winter sidewalk in Albuquerque and nearly blacked out when she saw her foot pointing the wrong way. She called me from the hospital for advice, because I, too, had recently broken my ankle.

Outside Pretoria in South Africa's Freedom Park, in the Sikhumbuto (place of remembrance), on the wall of 50,000 names, are names of 2,070 Cubans who died in Angola to defeat the South African army in 1976 at Quifandongo, and again in 1988, at Cuito Cuanavale.

"Ludlow Massacre," by Woody Guthrie, and a granite UMWA memorial on a patch of bare ground at the edge of the empty field.

I stopped for a woman broken down near Griffith Park, a big-boned older woman with stringy hair and a worn dress. Her kids had been playing in the roadside dirt—smudgy faces, snot running out of their noses and black, grubby fingers—I put her kids in the SUV with mine, threw her flat tire in the back, and she got in and we were off, looking for a gas station. How many times was that us, when we were little?

A hard orange light of late afternoon swept the sidewalks, cut long shadows across the avenues and shone from the walls of buildings. All of us in that light.

I love Wanda Coleman. But will someone please explain why each of these events are always on a weeknight?

because night time is the right time
because a pecan thinks like a walnut
because one night is as good as two lost years
because you can roll it and smoke it in that pipe mister
because you gotta limber up and reach out to your brothers and sisters
because out behind the bus depot they have a dance for people like
    yourself
because in a jiggle and a whiff things can change
because it's not all peanut butter and asphalt
because the wieners and dogs at pinks la brea are dreaming and
    steaming till late
because some airplanes go overhead and then for a long while that's all
    there was
because this is not poland 1939 and you can afford to live a little
because it could approach the key hour, the crucial one, the most
    important one, that one
because of the portable hand drill, the mounted cross bar, the steel
    flanged platform, and the overlook glasses
because of the grief, the bobbing joy, the overlooked grief, the still
    bobbing joy, the streaming desire
because of the murky swells glistening and shining under the
    dissipating fog

Eye Test

* Close your eyes, check all that apply in dreams.
___ 1. Star artichoke, broad expanse opening.
___ 2. American war, let's go old vacation.
___ 3. Wild radio of wire tumbleweeds, bow.
___ 4. Gold fish standing up for millions of Californias.
___ 5. Matte black intellectual grinding teeth.
___ 6. Collagist typewriter man + bicyclist womanish.
___ 7. Blatant white typewriter paper tens, nines.
___ 8. Bloody windshield evening beer ducks.
___ 9. Double, $5000 credit card I lunch with Thomas.
___ 10. Sigh rock portable forehead cardboard coughing.

*Open your eyes, check all who appear in the light.
___ 1. Miraculous viable tremendous shore-like mighty excellence.
___ 2. Poultry, highlighting the choice that is about to be made.
___ 3. Treetops of candles, which are going to stand for days ahead.
___ 4. Colliding with grease, windows close and doors shut or open.
___ 5. Something pointy, I should have written down this sentence.
___ 6. Mike Willard told me he rode his bike 57 miles aluminum-listening.
___ 7. Progress to Detroit, which rises in the manufacture of forgetting.
___ 8. Miraculous coats or jackets that felt dense to a body moment.
___ 9. Mock-style important-stamp over-radio lick-note spoil-if green-grip.
___ 10. Chop. Glowing.

* Look closely, check all that appear in lines beyond the figures.
___ 1. Mamayev Hill and Wounded Knee and the Cone of Disappearance
      and poemgranates and poem peaches and poem beetles.
___ 2. Thousands of dreams turning silver into hills and sweet breath
      cream, mild ointment.
___ 3. Logging wine bottles, dropping some on the other side of the Cone of
      Disappearance.
___ 4. Nagging dreams keep turning and sleeping while Calif. resumes
      foggy coastline at sunrise.

___ 5. How much was how much, 30 millions' sexual lives determined overall mountainous folds of the night.

___ 6. Shadows, cracks, or scratches caused upon my lenses, while nothing less than the glittering surface.

___ 7. Magdalen stairsteps where she swept off to sunlight, plausibly she is the Tree of Life.

___ 8. Widely poem bitch roiling poem pits whining poem tips tumbly poem pocks mostly.

___ 9. Fabric of darkness bright with the past. Folds whip along item survey lines.

___ 10. While I sorted the white socks, I did the dark laundry, remember.

the sky feels like the season is turning. i got a sweater. baby spider.
i always drive down huntington past the fire station at monterey pass
road, where ten or 15 years ago there was a brutal murder, some guy
with a shotgun followed two girls out of a party in boyle heights and shot
them to death in front of the fire station because it was said they broke
the mirror on his car. he chased them down and shot them one after the
other, screaming in the street in front of the station. i mentioned it at
the time when i got to school and a student said that one of them was
his aunt.

on the way to work this morning though i was thinking about the earth,
about the earth underneath the old railroad bed, under the parking lots
and office buildings, under the warehouses and the houses, does it love
us? does it feel us? is it listening? is it waiting for us to listen? maybe
these are questions for plants.

a big raven landed atop the streetlamp on the slope where huntington
turns into soto as i drove underneath. i thought it was a hawk but it was
a big raven. i thought there might be another smaller bird next to it but
i was going fast and over the hill by then.

it's the perfect spell, the perfect killing tool, the killing machine.

one million african americans are in u.s. prisons, 400,000 latinos.

they said the war on drugs was a war on the poor, because the institutions are inhabited by the apartheid imagination.

i place this line against the apartheid imagination.

the apartheid imagination requires no location, no physical body; because it has laws, records, court buildings, cells, conversations, and life.

it has radio programs, all-white movies, jailhouse mythologies, 2-D images.

before the latest killings started, it was there, and when the killers are forgotten, the apartheid imagination goes on thinking, dreaming up new killers.

who remembers the ones who killed emmett till, medgar evers, and fred hampton?

who remembers the guy who shot renisha mcbride?

who cares about aryan nation jason "gunny" bush, who executed jonathan bumstead of the aryan nation, also of wenatchee WA, for being a "race traitor," and who shot 9-year-old brisenia flores in the face in arivaca AZ?

who remembers the men of the 11th infantry brigade, who machine-gunned the women and children in the ditches of my lai? who remembers names of soldiers of the 7th cavalry who received the national medal of honor for slaughtering 300 men, women, and children at wounded knee?

who bothers to remember james earl ray?

who remembers the massacre sites of california?

i place this line in front of the images of trayvon martin, of jordan davis.

i place this line at the images of muhammad al-durrah, iman darweesh al hams, wajih ramahi.

i place this line alongside the images of abdulrahman al-awlaki and brisenia flores.

i place this line transparently over the names of jose antonio elena rodriguez, sergio hernandez guereca, ramses barron torres.

they were shot by the border patrol, walking or running, shot in the back.

they were killed by israeli forces using 3.1 billion dollars in 2013 u.s. military aid.

they were blown apart by a CIA drone firing a $70,000 agm-114 hellfire missile into a cafe.

they were killed by racists operating out of the apartheid imagination. the apartheid imagination was created by genocide against indians and by the slavery of africans as a construction designed to kill white conscience and memory.

anyone entering into the apartheid imagination is a white man or an indian or a rebel slave.

it uses a hegemony of all-white images to convince white people that any interest they may have is worth more than any life identified as other. it's a strong mechanism for killing people around the world like indonesia, rwanda, palestine, or india.

i have stood in the line for black and brown people at traffic court when i was the whitest one there, and the judge, an asian american guy substituting for the regular judge who was on holiday, let everyone go without a fine.

i have stood in my mom's kitchen window on a hill in city terrace and watched the pillars of smoke rising for days over the city of los angeles.

i have stood at the counter in the laundry of the men's county jail downtown in the fumes of dry cleaning chemicals handing out and collecting bags of laundry, have seen the faces of the men in line (where one guy always comes along trying to look like a stone killer and says, "pass me some fucking money or i will fuck you up," and maybe he was a stone killer, but i just returned his stare and took the next guy's bag).

i have waited in the plastic chairs and long lines of the DMV and i have seen who is waiting.

i've had lacerations cleaned out, my face x-rayed and patched up in the ER at county general hospital and seen who is waiting.

i have read poems in front of crowds of hundreds in universities from sf state to naropa, from university of minnesota to suny buffalo, and i have looked out on those faces and seen who is walking across the campus at hunters college and cal state fullerton, at the state colleges and the private colleges.

i have seen who is in the jail and in the court house line, who is waiting for a job outside home depot and orchard supply.

i've driven streets of towns of the hinterland where white teenagers scream something out of their cars and race away.

fuck the apartheid imagination, that's what i'm saying, death to the apartheid imagination and its english courses and its ideologies taught in the universities and churches, piss on the all-white movies pretending to be set in an all-white los angeles, all-white calif., all-white america, piss on the the norton anthology of post modern all white poetry and the norton anthology of all white american hybrid poetry, piss on all the little cliques of literati publishing all-white catalogs (with maybe one or 2 tokens) and touting another white guy as the latest wonderful thing (that thing is old, it's so old now), arnold schwarzenegger and ronald reagan were your fleeting white icons of pre-eminence, they were happy to see half my family, two generations, dispossessed and sent to live in horse stalls of santa anita racetrack and colorado river internment camps, happy to go along with lives being destroyed, happy to sign some apology letters decades later, to put up a few plaques on historical sites out in the desert.

who remembers individuals operating behind the poison alzheimer's of the apartheid imagination?

who shall remember the mushroom cloud of the apartheid imagination when the next killers are shooting, murdering a child in the headlines, and the people post and repost all the images, talking laws, discussing footnotes and factoids?

the names are in the ground, the apartheid imagination like a shadow above them.

i place this line in front of it saying my whole life has been against it, and the rest of my life will be against it.

i place this line in front of it.

Postcard of Dust

I've been gone for a month, and when I return in January, dust motes swirl in the bathroom window light. Dust bunnies pile in corners around my bed. I haven't been around—nobody has come in or out—where does it all come from? Some vortex, crack in the universe I can't see? This town seems fresh in winter, chilly breezes and rain. But the rugs are saturated with dust. A fuzzy softness wafts in the sunshine in oblong rectangles from the windows. Maybe it comes from my mind, from a lifetime of crummy thoughts? From the daily crude sledgehammering of ideas on the rocks and stones of dullness, stupidity, and bullshit? Maybe it's released, minute by minute, from these books? That can't be it.

Ah, there's the broom.

pot of beans boiling or simmering, reading about beans or thinking
about beans, beans of thoughts, little heads of beans, Anasazi beans
and sangre de toro beans, black beans of little eyes of small animals,
beans cleaned of debris and rocks, dirt, beans that taste of earth
and steam, with sliced pan-fried anaheim or hatch chiles, "lost all
patience for people who primarily think about food, particularly their
own. it's solopsistic and boring," cara b. said on facebook, i met her
on the top floor of a big hotel overlooking the zocalo in mexico city,
where i clomped out on the balcony on crutches, ankle broken from
backpacking cascades in northern washington, we were there with a
bunch of writers, harry gamboa, ruben martinez, reed johnson, karla
diaz & mario ybarra, luis valdez, tom hayden sneering early in the
morning as we gathered for nice breakfast buffet on the high balcony
across from Palacio Nacional, we're all just beans, beans simmering or
boiling in our pots, together or alone, steam of thoughts rising in the
kitchen of the world, on the fires of desire, on the wings of heat, red
beans, pintos, cooking those beans not bullets, paper beans and beans
of electric words, not for killing anyone, not suicidal, but simple—rip a
tortilla in half, eat some beans

Taylor's Question

—how do you survive, how do you make it through?

Always listen to the women.

My father broke my mother's nose, her hand.
But he didn't die alone. Two of my sisters were there,
holding his hand.

Driving down the street, you make a sudden maneuver to dodge a stalled
vehicle, and the guy on your tail flips a switch when you cut him off,
speeds up and cuts in front of you, screaming and flipping you off,
jams on his brakes so his bumper comes up on your vehicle,
you're swerving out of the lane to evade, speeding to pass
in the traffic on the avenue—dusk falling—you're laughing
because he speeds up, both vehicles beginning to race;
a woman's voice rises to a pitch: "No, no, no!"

And you're reluctant, but already you're slowing.

Listen.

For Ryan and Umeko

2 in the rain sheets of caffeine and ecstasy, shivering in feathery yellows
of muskeg.
2 riding garish summer blue of joy and intent, riding and peering down deep
green swells.
2 in furled sheets of pink dawns, rooms of northern light shine thru flesh
like smoke.
2 in the automative spaces of swollen USA, driving the mind's clean speeds.
2 in the shivering sedges and rushes, whose passions verge like timbered
slopes.
2 in abrupt exaltations of the morning, voices from the radio fading like
tenderness fades.
2 along the sunset shore of wine and dreams, snapping twigs and branches
into a fire.
2 by the lanky dog in a flock of sanderlings, where kettle or kettling is a word
meaning a flock that flies up in unison, wheeling and swerving.
2 at the edge of a rolling, tumbling Pacific, where yellowlegs, sanderlings,
and sandpipers fling themselves up at Knot and at dusk.
2 in the virtual numbers of the digital world, where algorithms of skin
smell warm.
2 , we know which 2, not like a pair of hands, a pair of shoes or anything else,
or even 2 droplets falling out of a sky full of rain or a night full
of stars.
Those 2, they know better than we.

Long ago I joined the cult of womb-weary midwives, signed the membership form of that woman walking the sidewalk crack of weariness between her eyes, stood at the end of the line with the discount crowd waiting their turn to pay off ghost children hanging on them, I too walked in the shadow of the the ficus trees at the Italian Hall and the CPUSA storefronts and the dirty palm trees, today I submit my vote for the Tzotzil and Quiche day laborers for president of the association and its 30,000 members, standing together with you, speaking softly into a cup of black coffee in our four hands or in our eight hands, under the vast Western tent of blood-pink weariness in the sunset before the endless infinite universe, there I keep the brochure of their society in my pocket, already paid my dues to the International Brotherhood of Electrical Firefighters and Sanitationary Workers, walking that line that goes out the door, across the parking lots in lines of taillights and headlights, dispersing throughout the city to deliver you this ticket. Sign here _____ .

1.
Jose Felicito Figueroa Gutierrez, I walked his western concrete
sidewalk

Catarino Gonzalez Merino, I walked underneath urban ficus branches
he pruned

Mateo Salgado Perez, I walked by his painted storefront, "LICUADOS
NATURALES PROBIOTICOS JUGOS BIONICOS PARA SALUD," perky
portraits of spiky flamboyant fruits

Chelve Benitez Jaramillo, I took them from his fingertips and bit firm
whitish fleshy strawberries at the farmers market, $4

Rogelio Dominguez Benitez, I lit the sacks of mesquite charcoal he
trucked from his state, sending flames and sparks up in the dark

Hector Ramirez Robles, I admired his variegated folds of multicolored
hues, processes unfolding and shifting

Jorge Mauricio Torres Herrera, fuzzy 15-year-old mustache, I know his
wry glint, wondering about his empty chair 2 days

Roberto Rivera Gámez, sanded bookshelves, built and finished them in
the garage and let them dry

Serafin Rivera Gámez, I like the way his life is a broad avenue of
marvelous lives, exchanged and relayed across blue light of oceanic
distances

Elisendo Cabanas González, I know women he was working for, women
he supported year in year out, looking out for—unfailing—their finite
and infinite joys possible

Marco Antonio Villaseñor Acuña, 5, I was privileged to move through any day that was heartened by his heart, that was brightened by his gaze, that was sweetened with his breath

José Antonio Villaseñor Acuña, brushing my teeth with the lime-green toothbrush recycled from plastics he processed

Edgar Gabriel Hernández Zúñiga, I peeled and ate the orange he handed to me

Juan Carlos Castillo Loredo, he passed between me and the sun, looking over the sun on the ocean

Ricardo González Mata, he built buildings that I walked through in October, to the second floor of the Science Library at the University of California, Riverside to read poems

Oscar González Guerrero, my vehicle necessarily runs on parts he delivered, while I believe he's reflected in a cloud along the San Gabriel Mountains

José Luis Ramirez Bravo, his touch folded inside clothes I happen to wear, fabric on skin

Juan José Morales, swallowing coffee from hills in his homeland, might've been his suggestion that I wake up

Augusto Stanley Vargas, it was his cash I received in change, I put those coins into a parking meter that didn't work

2.
i took his notion i noticed her fillip
i thank her for regional fusion i was swayed by the tenuous assurances
     across the avenue
i marched with one million may first
he cut my hair
he set my vistas aright

they were both quiche i bought them lunch
she made the tamales of the past and the tamales outside time
they filled the playground with signs of life
she made everyone's skin glow with sunset at bolsa chica state beach
he punched the button in the elevator he swabbed my arm and took my
    blood
"relax your fist now," he said
(my blood has been tested, it was found to be basically exactly the same)
"just hold that for a moment," he said

strawberry

when we had hot water in our veins I was kissing her nose that was
also running it tasted of salty strawberries her dog was barking above
noises we were making I was telling it to shut up it was vibrating like
a strawberry I was nibbling from lips or fingertips of somebody who
had crossed a desert to walk up my street and deliver it whose seagulls
banked and soared in a guttering breeze sands flapping in the gusts
of crows when we had sugar and salt on our skin chewing leafy parts
licking lemony fresh tendrils when we both had blisters you could
peel and reveal whitish red flesh like strawberries sleeping like any old
person in daylight

I saw dad sitting on the porch of the rooming house on 6th Street, San Jose. Leaning back in a ratty chair with a tall can in his hand, he hadn't shaved or cut his hair in months. I saw him before he saw me, staring off at a distant point. When he fixed on my face as I crossed the yellow lawn, he recognized me and grinned.

I saw Mario Ybarra standing in the center line of Sunset Boulevard at dusk, between lines of streaming traffic. I yelled "Hey Mario!" driving by, but I don't think he heard me.

I saw Selene Santiago at the Alhambra farmers market, and when I turned around, she was gone.

In a warm summer drizzle in Manhattan, somebody said, "I heard someone call out your name." I stepped off the corner at the corner of 5th and 34th and looked up and down the avenue between skyscrapers at the crowd emerging through corridors of plywood and scaffolding, flowing across the intersection in four directions, but I recognized no one.

At the Public Theater in Manhattan, on my way to see Roger Guenver Smith's solo play, "A Huey P. Newton Story," I got in the elevator and Roger entered. "Hey Roger," I said, and he said, "How are you?"

Jimmy Lew had been a runner in high school, and now on the trail to Vernal Falls at dawn in the Yosemite Valley, he rushed ahead of me. I hurried to keep up, breathing hard, lungs aching in the frozen air, trying to keep him in sight as he zigzagged the icy trail above.

My brother told me that the last time he saw Zeus Gaytan he was on TV, wearing the blue helmet of a UN peacekeeper in Bosnia. The last time I saw him was in the 1980s, in the Japanese garden on the rooftop of the New Otani Hotel, talking about people we never saw.

I had the wife and kids in the pickup truck; we'd visited one of my wife's college friends, who was working as a public defender in San Jose, then drove downtown to 6th Street, where my father lived in a rooming house. He didn't have a phone. He didn't know we were in town. One of the boarders, whose name was maybe Kevin (he'd mentioned other boarders in his frequent letters), said my father was out, but he'd tell him we had come by. My wife said maybe we could return to see if he was in later. As we turned to get back in the truck, my father crossed the street and met us. He was drunk and looked like he hadn't slept at home in days. In fact, he said, he'd spent the week "across town with the Indians." I could see him trying to shake off the drunkenness, to get a grip on himself internally. "Just a minute," he said, walking over to vomit into the shrubbery. "Are you all right?" I asked. "I just need a cup of coffee," he said. And it was true. He heated coffee on the stove in a tiny kitchen, drank two cups, and was ready to meet his grandchildren.

I saw Harry Gamboa in the Fremont Avenue Alhambra Starbucks; as I entered, he saw me and rose to say hello. I saw Harry in the Mexico City Starbucks off the zocalo.

Dad grew angry when we said we all had to be quiet because the kids were going to bed. "I've never been treated so badly in my life!" he exclaimed as he stalked down the stairs and away through the trees, a twelve pack in a sack under his arm.

The first time I saw Lawrence Ferlinghetti, I was walking toward City Lights Bookstore and saw him arranging books in the window.

I saw Rick Harsch sitting on my balcony, smoking and drinking a beer. He emitted anxious smoke like my brother.

I saw a raven clucking and burbling in a tree in the Yosemite Creek Campground. Later, a raven, maybe it was the same one, was taking a dust bath in the dirt road.

I saw Ernesto Cardenal under the eaves of the fairgrounds in Managua where we went for the First International Nicaraguan Book Fair.

The U.S. booth consisted of a consortium of small presses, including Children's Book Press of San Francisco, Calyx Press of Oregon, Curbstone Press of Connecticut, and West End Press of Albuquerque. The Cubans and Mexico had big booths the next aisle over. Across the aisle, facing the U.S. stall and its improvised shelves and tables, were the Iranians, with their giant laminated photographs of dead torture victims of the U.S.-supported SAVAK strung like sheets on a clothes line next door to the North Koreans, with their immaculate white booth that housed one shelf of books, the collected works of Kim Il-sung, underneath his smiling portrait. Sandinista Minister of Culture Cardenal toured the stalls, saying hello. I thanked him for hosting us, and especially for his own poetry, which I said was crucially important to me. Later I met Cardenal's British translator, who said his books only sold a few hundred copies in the U.S.

Out on the flat Sea of Cortez, the broad back of the whale (a blue whale) broke the surface like the inverted black steel hull of a ship underwater, black and smooth and shining, with a kind of nub on the crest line down the center as it arched its back and swam on.

I saw Carlo Pedace sitting on my sister's back porch, smoking. We'd first met Carlo in Naples in 1978, and now his hair was gray, but he looked good. Three generations of distant family gabbed around him, but he was thinking of something else. He looked like he was waiting.

I saw my grandmother Alberta Northway sitting on her couch alone in her apartment in Santa Barbara.

In line at the airport in Philadelphia, I saw my co-worker (Doctor) Joe Cocozza enter the line behind me. He introduced me to his partner.

I saw him at the table of professors with Karen Yamashita. I had walked into the cafe looking for lunch, and when Robert Allen started talking about the Port Chicago explosion and mutiny, I told him, "Robert, we met in Nicaragua more than twenty years ago," and we laughed and hugged. He had talked about the 1944 Port Chicago explosion and mutiny case in Nicaragua twenty years earlier. "I learned about Port Chicago from you," I said, "In fact, you're the only person I've ever heard talk about it."

I saw Willie Herron walking down the long hill on Eastern Avenue by the Dolores Canning Company, toward Floral.

I saw the yucca spike was a light golden blonde, its seed pods rattling like earrings, halfway between the heavy reptilian green of its emergence and the last, blasted, desiccated, hollow black stalk it would become.

call it any pitted faded word, what you saw

tenderly sometimes, moist hollow of collarbone, call it covered in sage
dusk or rusty drip faucet

gaze darkly glancing inside and outside, call it potato skin or thrift of
main street lights

mystery of clean neat cuticles and knuckle creases, call it loose sailing
spider thread or glance at the storm front

hair sheen taken in hand or ends flicked back, call it thudding of the
earth or several short pencils

voice turns the corner and leans over your shoulder, call it mild surmise
in error or shape rising like a wave

arcs of shoulder profile and light on cheekbone, call it scattering of tern
cries or lick on a postage stamp

curl or fold at the top of the ear seen and noted, call it unknown
automobile that once passed or windblown letters

and the palm (held up) that looks so human like all of history, call it
palm held (up) in mid-air or bleeding across an edge

and the bones of the face and the skull strong as an idea, call it
afternoon's dryers open warm or edge of moss

and tendon in the neck and a vein in the neck, call it summer's past dust
of trails or city of every freeway

and reflection of it and remembering it, re-imagined it (as nothing), call
that pity's sweat or bits of bread rolled into balls with fingertips

Valentina Tereshkova Postcard

Little universes!———What's U. doing? She went out, took the dog
out 90 minutes ago———I sent her a rocket ship piloted by Valentina
Tereshkova, cosmonaut, to land beside her with roar of smoke and
blasted dust, Valentina steps from the ship, shakes hands, "Comrade!"
———M., who at this moment is driving north on what highway, to Santa
Ynez, Valentina can scout out her Toyota truck far below through wispy
clouds, shining Southern Calif. day, slight haze———zooming over the
Toyota truck, Valentina sets down with expertise and precision, out of
some other time, some other ideology, some other dimension, Valentina
can say hello to M. from all of us, and then———What's Grandma up to?
Sudoku? Reading? ———Lift-off! Zoom! Valentina greets you with
comradely outer space greetings from U. and M., and all of us!———
J. and C. are dabbling at their computers, working, it seems, at the
kitchen table———D. joins them with her computer———Valentina
could set her rocket ship down adroitly in the driveway, the whole house
would shake, dust drifts from the ceiling, the door bell rings!———
Who's there? ———Valentina!

Where did I put it? Can I get there across the untethered plank? How
old are the planks of the rotting walkway, leading up from the dock
(with the sunken yacht, bridge black with mold)? How wide is this
island? How parenthetical is one last appositive? How is it I feel the
shadow cutting silent across the mudflat, cutting across the flat green
water? How does the deep opacity of green refract blades of sunglare
into my useless old thoughts? How about these nails sticking out? How
about the rocks in the mudflats, the moss in the trees? How shall I fall
through the next fifteen minutes? How to drop down through the hole
rotten in the deck to the pilings underneath, thence to proceed across
the rocks, slippery below? How to find the overgrown trails they had to
have used? How about the shiny commercial mixer on the counter of
the abandoned kitchen where the roof had fallen in, except on that part
that looked like the kitchen was still in use? How about the bedroom, all
motel beige, burnt sienna, olive green, coverlet on the beds made, lamp
on the nightstand and everything under thick dust, maritime print on
the wall warping? How about algae sliming the opening of the concrete
reservoirs? How about the shack at the end of the walkway, looking
out on the silent cove (with one dock sunken between rotting pilings,
the water deep, deep green, black against the uplifted black rock of the
island), shattered glass and shattered white ceramic plates littering
the floor? Will it tug at my thinking like gristle, like a ligament, when it
comes, the call?

chico postcard

i was dropped off on a long highway that turned into an avenue with two huge boxes, each about the size of a kitchen table, and one extra suitcase. it was very late, which is to say, in the predawn hours, so the streets were largely empty, and the house where i was going was on top of the hill somewhere, the hill dense with apartment buildings and houses under street lamps and stars, through which wound narrow streets. the boxes were not heavy at all, i could carry one at a time, but there was no way to carry two at a time and a suitcase besides. as usual, i had to figure out a way. then i awoke in chico, calif. on a chilly morning at the thunderbird motel as the sunshine slanted down main street and melted the frost. and i had no boxes and no suitcase to carry, and everything was better already.

Mother's Day, night

SOMEWHERE IN THERE, the streets I know end in vagueness, generalities. Somewhere in there, the streets of the city and the streets of night end in a spicy, smoky smell of girl sweat, like bread fresh from the oven. Somewhere in there, our decades together, decades we've known each other. As if those decades still exist; in fact they do not. Phone messages erased from numbers that never existed in this century, messages she wished I would have received, once upon a time. However many times she saved my life, two or three at least, her unspoken fears or disgust with me must exist somewhere in there like shadows at night. Shadows on the other side of shrubbery, under the dim glare of a semi-distant streetlamp. Darkness, unknowing, on the far side of walls, the other side of eyes. I walk the night streets and avenues in sleep, in dreams. I drive them, talking to her. Everything that was done and undone, even if it's gone now. Years vanished as if they never were, but her smell rises in my memory, volatile as gasoline, the dense female fragrance I kiss at the base of her spine. It rises behind the daylight, like a mole rubbed between two fingertips, like a big river coming around a bend in the dark.

Probably you were making love a couple times, you were getting busy.

Laying sod, planting trees, paving a walkway. Perhaps you called your
    mother.

Perhaps your child. Driving from L.A. to the Mexican border can take what.

The estimate for the bathroom, 15 to 20K. What's the weather going to be
    like when you arrive?

Something about Gaza. The woman's car in the intersection...

You parked, and by the time you got there, two other guys showed up to
    help push.

Rutsu 18, or Tokoro in S. Pasadena? Bombed-out buildings like from
    World War II, gray concrete dust.

Gray concrete dust on survivors. The Israelis.

News on in another room; saturated arena colors of a flat screen in a
    sports bar, Washington DC?

Dim sports bar? A toddler cradled in a hunched father's arms, missing the
    top of the head.

How much had you? How much more to drink? Two or three maybe.

Phrase, tit for tat, something like that. It canceled out. How much money
    was it to you?

New appliances, developments in robotics, software versus hardware. Debt.

How's traffic? How's it look? If you peeked and saw Gaza, you saw it.

You saw the end of your world, your own death in a way, the limit of sighs.

A breath, your own, and someone talking, saying something you didn't
    quite catch.

Hedges, fences, and trees as you drive on. Houses, neighborhoods of night
    streets. Little universes.

Living in the Community, Focusing On Social Justice Postcard

1. vote democratic, burble like the ravens, chortle like the crows
2. pay your taxes and your dues, eat sunshine ravenous
3. comb your hair, wear clothing large enough for the body, live jumping
4. organize the workers, organize your face
5. encourage fellow feeling, recognize humanity's wheelbarrow
6. take leadership, hop pertly about the landscape with wings folded back
7. never say die, bleed like the new girl
8. drink plenty of water, die on time
9. read theory, throw rocks into intersecting dimensions
10. fresh air and exercise, flange the electric guitar of nose and ear cartilage
11. don't burn plastic, listen to waves squall and spit
12. women equal, attend all the conferences of rumor and haste
13. don't swear, swearing up and down the high seas
14. fill what's empty, empty what's full, torn flap
15. be gentle, spoon the earthquake and tsunami
16. do your homework, squander Squanto
17. be bold, bolt your teeth with blackened modernism
18. don't be a sucker, don't play that cardamom
19. drive safe, not on trees in orange light

Ragazzi

I hear them before I see them from across the parking lot, hooting
and calling out on the street, two boys on skateboards surging up
Main Street, another boy on a bike ahead of them, heading west
toward Fremont.

I emerge from the sliding glass doors of the market with my sack of
soup vegetables.

I never get a clear glimpse of them, don't really look at them as I cross
the parking lot. I feel like I already know them, so I don't even bother
to look.

I am shifting the sack of goods from one arm to another as I walk,
avoiding a Smartcar turning at me, reaching for my keys with my free
hand, already making my soup in my mind after 3 days of a bad cold
or flu. But I have registered them as they rush lanes of traffic on Main
Street to the opposite side. I like how their boyish shouts rebuke my
indifferent silence.

They cross the twilight median under the big ficus trees for the far
sidewalk.

They cross over into twilight shadows, like figures of speech in some
poem.

Like flying horsemen or like ravens, like this or like that metaphor, boys
with the changeable energy of boys, like figures gesticulating in dreams
or like the boys we once were. Rushing out into the horizons of their
own lives like pronghorns.

Crossing into twilight shadows I don't even distinguish let alone really
see, the boys like ragazzi in the background, extras in some black and
white 1960s Italian movie.

But partly I am listening to their voices, which have crossed over to the other side.

No break in traffic, no emergency screech or sound of accident, twilight assumes the flow into evening. I set the sack on the passenger seat, drive out of the lot. I catch a last glimpse of them out of the corner of my eye as I pass, the bicyclist keeping pace with the skaters in front of the boxing club and the Jehovah's Witness churchfront, heading toward Carroll's Brake Service, but already I'm ahead. They're just half-seen figures barely inscribed inside a couple lines here; they're on their way and passed far beyond, throwing giant shadows across a blue evening.

Ode 2

—for Eetalah and Carissa

2 in the rain sheets of minneapolis, shivering in ecstasy and caffeine.
2 in the garish noon of bakersfield, shivering in joy and terror.
2 in the basin and ranges of nevada, delivering joy or terror.
2 in the national stadium of chile, american agents stalking.
2 in the liquified muskeg of SE alaska, shivering slightly stalking.
2 in the mild whorishness of the city, shivering in joy and exaltation.
2 in the purposive burning of civilizations, lost in flesh of smoke.
2 in the hurtling automotive spaces of USA, wracked with joy or fear.
2 in the rising and falling motion of the Pacific, rolling and trembling.
2 in the shopping blocks of downtown boulder, talking poetry and stuff.
2 in the long avenues and boulevards of L.A., cleaning properties.
2 in the pink, furled sheets of bedroom, trembling as sleep falls.

Wendy, Jimmy, and I were talking about you (though you remain unknown to us), and salamanders, baby rats, tadpoles, lupines, and condors.

We hiked through underbrush of poison oak in redwood groves on the creek in Soberanes Canyon, recounting how far we got with John and Paul.

We talked about winter rain, about (unknown) houses, (unknown) rocks, (unknown) time and the trail, and (unknown) you. Talking about all the unknown things.

Dry, rocky high slopes on the ridge were furred by this year's rains, furred with invasive grasses like rattlesnake grass.

Prickly silver thistle stems bent under coronas of whitish spikes and rich violet petals, Wendy touched the wild (dense) purple delphinium.

The briza maxima drooped everywhere their shiny greenish rattlesnake rattles. Winds whirled out of the sky at hand.

At the rock outcrop, Jimmy said his iPhone said we were 975 feet above the sea; we ate sandwiches overlooking the broad ocean crashing on the rocky shore with a distant cloudbank obscuring the far horizon (Wendy said she heard sea lions, and I listened)—turkey buzzards and redtail hawks above.

We had not stopped talking about housing foreclosures, government support for Goldman Sachs, Lehman Brothers, AIG, the bankers who destroyed the economy—it was facilitated and nothing done to prevent it—they make the wars go on and on, the kids are told to make their lives in the devastated economy in a shrunken, withering culture.

Grass on the high slopes marked with California poppies (poison oak cannot abide the dry, rocky slopes)—there's a protein in black Western fence lizard blood that kills Lyme disease from ticks—(sunning) living and dead lizards on the trail (the ticks live off the lizards that eat millions; Wendy said she's seen lizards with ticks on them)—they go together. We described it as we talked about your (unknown) time.

the fish is the Soviet Union of rolling fields — the sunrise is the milk sap fig of my neighbor's loneliness — the belly is the rotund nation of toys — the basil is the creamy Arctic flap of blue spruce — the salty finger is the Jen Hofer of friendly shade — the curve in the road is the unremitting Saturday of 2013 — the life of trees is the Doughnut Hole of remote understanding — the maroon stain is the common humanity of total moon — the desiccated pool is the real waterfall of nodding simple —

Ketchikan Postcard

at noon, 6 or 8 harleys parked in front of the house, the riders standing about. one of them had apparently gone off the road because of a four-year-old boy standing in the highway. the boy (whom we did not see) was unharmed and untouched. in the afternoon, i walked grateful through the forest of hemlock, spruce, and cedar, and now that darkness has fallen, i go on into that dark, grateful still.

"There must be a pony!" Postcard

The tripod is mustard, and it's rainy.
The famous tower is fruit, and petals falling.
The vertical arm is swaths, and hair warmth.
The aluminum throat is Filipinas, and Arizona dirt.
The window champion is bold, and riffing darling bolt.
Suspicious juniper of gray must, and the general information.
Someone stretched out a marvelous hand.

for julia

drink this glass of wine that the broken glass rights itself in the
hand and the cracks vanish from the crystal, that the shattered glass
reassembles inside bright furnace and inert sand, that the stain flies up
from the floor and sinks into the liquid like refracted light, that the juice
flows through the grapes and vine and the leaf-borne dew of another
season, that the storm-wrecked thing on the sand flies tonight as a gull,
that the hard rain soaks the debris and stumps of the clearcut, and when
clouds descend, there emerges the forest without end.

how is the artist or writer to function (survive and produce)
in the community, outside of institutions?

1. all you mfa candidates, all you college students, all you awp hangers-
on, all you high school students wondering what to do (which is the same
thing as how to live, how to make a life of your own, how to save your own
life), all you secret poets looking for support, all you striving artists who
need a job, what about you?

2. most will sooner or later find themselves outside institutionalization.

3. dreams tell us that the life of the mind goes on regardless. regardless of
institutions or individuals, the life of the mind is a collective dreaming. the
dream goes on, whether or not anyone is making movies and documenting
it, holding conferences and seminars about it. the mind goes on.

4. the institutional imagination, with its schedules and regulations, with
its tests and prerequisites, will be insufficient on the outside, in a broader
world of completely indifferent and more democratic sidewalks, offices,
transactions, atmospheres. it's true that sometimes high school or college
provides the only encouragement working-class students receive for
creative thinking. but unlike academia, which scaffolds individual efforts
and conceives of art and writing as individualistic practices, the broader
world is indifferent. institutions fetishize rational discourse, operating
on the level of rationalization, as if sitting around a conference table
in negotiation is going to be a major life skill for you. perhaps not! an
institutionalized aesthetic production process you may have formulated
in academia may not work for you outside.

5. you must get outside and feel all right, producing some creativity that
can stand the daylight (and the smog).

6. you may perhaps object that "the community" lacks community; in fact,
there seem to be people there who are actively hostile, perhaps violent,
toward "art," "dreams," "poetry," etc. you may object that in academia or
other institutions, where there are rules for discourse and behavior, you

didn't feel exposed to hostility. but for all its talk (all of its attention to crossing t's and dotting i's), little dreaming occurs in academia and institutionalized civil forums. they emphasize rationalizations; their discussions take place inside bureaucratic mythologies. the creative thinking found there may be mostly recycled early 20th-century concepts.

7. in the community (that lacks community), some may feel hostile. there may be violence. many have been defeated; they feel they have been defeated. but that doesn't stop their dreaming, mythologizing, their visions. make no mistake, millions of people that the media and Hollywood depict as nobodies and extras in the background (people of color) or zombies or killers (working-class people), they are dreaming, too. all of which helps you to figure out how to survive as an artist, writer, dreamer, mythologist, person of vision. stay alive. don't get hurt. make a living, a commitment to the community that you make while you are doing it, while you are producing.

how to survive?

a. call me. call me at one AM, crying so i can hear mucus over the line, say UC irvine decided in the middle of the first year of your MFA program to take back your financial award.

b. talk to me late into the night even if i have to get up for work.

c. meet me for noodles; i'll take you to pho. i'll listen to your whole deal, how you're a tenured professor but your books don't sell. you edited a poetry series that was canceled by the university in a budget cut.

d. i'll buy you pho.

e. ask me to lend you $40. i will.

f. text me. say you're going to be at the airport on such and such a date, layover for the afternoon. i'll take you to aliki's tavern greek restaurant.

g. meet me at the little house in el sereno, your relatives standing silent behind us on the porch in the darkness before dawn, duffel bags in hand. we'll embrace out front, breath coming out plumes in the chill. they slept on the floor and they're ready to go, so there's not much time to to chat. you don't need more coffee, just a drink of water. you got thousands of miles to drive.

h. we'll help you load. your people are waiting on you.

i. call me when you get to california. tell me you just arrived and don't know anyone. you don't have a place to stay. i'll give you my cousin's number (this was before he was married).

j. my cousin will let you stay at his place, mid-city for a month till you get a place. usually i've got a couch or an extra room.

k. meet me by accident at the front door. i'll be living in a different house by then. one night when i am cleaning out the empty house, having moved out, trash bags in both hands, i can't see you under the street lamp. people stand at the bottom of the stairs by the street lamp. you step into the light and tell me who you are, and we laugh because i haven't seen you in years, the last time was a thousand miles away. you're looking for an address up the street, a meeting at a house of an old revolutionary.

l. i'll point up the dark street. i might know the person you are looking for.

m. change your name. get rid of your slave name, revert to the indigenous. run a pirate radio station out of a van around the hilltops of east l.a. broadcasting secret revolutionary communiques in the middle of the night.

n. ask me for a letter of recommendation for a job at the university. send me the CV, i'll say anything. i'll be glad to. that's why they call it "creative writing." i've written hundreds of rec letters.

o. ask me to show up and talk to your students. i will.

p. i'll drive to nimitz middle school and read poems to a library full of middle schoolers. i'll read them poems and answer their questions about poems and about how to be a writer. i'll find a ticket on my windshield afterwards. ask me to speak to a group of high school kids at the alternative high school. i'll read them a couple of poems at the picnic table under the tree. i'll give each one at the table a free book of poems and sign the ones who ask. (marisela norte will talk to students at another table.) ask me to talk to students at ucr (graduate seminars and undergrads on their cell phones), university of minnesota, harvard, hunter college, columbia, occidental, ucsd, ucsc, sf state, suny buffalo, eerie community college (where those kids paid real attention and asked great questions), pasadena city college, bisbee central school project, cal state l.a., cal state northridge, i'll go. i'll drive a rental car from boston south, from tucson through tombstone to bisbee, i'll drive a rental from the airport at cedar rapids to a reading at lacrosse WI, up the cold winter mississippi river to minneapolis. i'll drive four hours south through hellish stop and start traffic on the 5 to get to a benefit reading in someplace like laguna beach or san clemente.

q. ask me to meet you so we can talk about grad school.

r. ask me to meet you so we can talk about teaching writing to students.

s. ask me to meet you so we can talk about your manuscript, publishers, agents, your options.

t. don't hesitate to appear in my dreams:
...california coast town, some novices—community college group—a handful of people amid desultory scattering of student desks, what's going on? nothing? the instructor, who is a pal, who doesn't have programming or an agenda, turns to me, "you want to read something? you got something?" of course. i always have something, i can always do something. i'll read "the blue garage." but what is "the blue garage"? it was supposed to be something i could run through without thinking, but now i can't recall exactly what it was. i just need something, just a little clue, a word would suffice, just to get started. hold on, i'll do this. i got this. but i can't remember what it was. it's like everything has gone

dark, and indeed i am standing in the middle of the blue garage. it's an
old abandoned garage, debris, blue paint blistered and peeling, and
i've been standing there so long only one person's left, my host leads me
away. there's a reception or gathering afterward in some little downtown
storefront, but i'm in no mood, disgusted with myself, later i wake up in a
furniture store in a pile of rugs—it's morning in the town, time to go.

u. when you get old and sick, someone will put out the call. this person has been one of our best, one of our bravest, one of our toughest, they stood up for us, they spoke up, and now they're old and sick and need our help. because it's true (you were brave and you never stopped), i'll cut a check.

v. though i have debt without end, i'll write a check.

w. ask me what i do for a living. when i answer, frown with your disgust and class bias. "really? that's what you do?" you stare at me for a beat, eyes hooded. other people are friendly all around the table but after that exchange, you're cold. what upsets you? (maybe you're one of those professors who couldn't publish a book to save your life.) are you one of those positivists, whose rationales mask horror at the seeming physical indifference of the world? if you cared to talk about it, i'd suggest that more than bureaucratic positivism is required to write or make art. believe me, i worked two jobs for decades to enable my writing.

x. come over to my house to tell me you can't stand it where you're staying because the poet hosting you in l.a. fights all the time with her boyfriend—"it's a house of pain." talk to me about all the poetry festivals you attend around the world, where can you read your poems in los angeles, and how can you get money for your poetry? i'll tell you what i know about festivals, small presses, gigs, the poetry business. invite me to read poems in new zealand, as long as i pay my way.

y. call me and leave a message saying you want me to look at your manuscript.

z. i'll be happy to look at your manuscript. don't commit suicide in that motel in san clemente. don't treat other people like they are disposable, least of all yourself! don't throw yourself away! treat people well, be good to yourself, be at your best in your work, and you will receive coffee, grants, awards, blurbs, introductions, couches to sleep on, beer, wine, meals, job offers, referrals, advice, sexual favors, puppies, flowers, photographs, poems, rides, money, fellowships, lessons, trips, tips, applause, passes, residencies, walks, recipes, bicycles, admiration and respect, hugs, stories, glimpses, visions, and gifts of lives that otherwise would never come your way. if you commit suicide in that motel room, you get nothing.

one of the beautiful things about art or writing can be that it comes from you, represents you in the crowd, bears your handprint, it tells your story, it's personal in the indifferent universe, it's fun in such grim times, the hopeful thing that is your own gift to give. when you survive as an artist or writer, you will produce art and writing that will help you to survive.

so:

1. meet the artists and writers of your community. talk to your elders. tell them why their work has been important to you. to do that, you must find out why their work is important to you. who are your predecessors? find out how they did it. ask them how it went for them.

2. meet the people in your community. talk to the elders. find out how they have used intelligence and creativity to survive as human beings, which is to say, how did they survive creatively, intellectually? you want to survive as a human being, with creativity and intelligence.

3. which is also to say, how do artists and writers relate to and depend on people in the community? how do artists and writers relate to the tamale lady, community activists, labor organizers, busybodies, gossipers, to the Executive Secretary-Treasurer of the Los Angeles County Federation of Labor, AFL-CIO, to homeless people, to the store clerk, (to the video-store clerk who wants to be a poet and his co-worker, the video-store clerk who wants to be a sculptor), to ghosts, to secret and forgotten individuals of the past, to kids (who in a few

years will be completely different people)? how do artists and writers relate to members of informal underground organizations, to gangs, to businesses, to soccer coaches in the city parks and teachers at the nearby school, to the retiree who grew up around here before there were houses, who used to teach judo in Boyle Heights, whose sister is a well-known artist, now he has Alzheimer's? many of these people know the secrets of survival and how to create community. their survival and their triumphs show that. the life of the community shows that, vibrating on those frequencies.

in short, I suggest that you must develop community, you must create for yourself community, beyond just a "support network." Recently, in the typical superficial style of *L.A. Magazine*, like all such booster magazines devoted to only the glossiest, most superficial view of the city, a former *L.A. Times* writer, Scott Timberg, wrote an essay called "Leaving Los Angeles" in which he mourns the cumulative effects of Reagonomics and the destruction of the "middle class" in L.A. and particularly his own deteriorated status. "As much as I like Los Angeles," Timberg writes, "which has been 'home' longer than my Maryland hometown was—I'm no longer willing to be a third-class citizen here."

(I say that America has always treated its artists and writers as third-class citizens.)

Perhaps you, like Timberg, grew up believing that you could move to any community anywhere and, due to your education, your whiteness, your privilege, you could engage in a "middle-class" life (where every activity is a business transaction allowed by your money and monetized skills, neatly performed within the snappy ideologies of capitalism) and generally not have to consider the struggles of people in your community—and specifically, the struggles of people who made the community more liveable for everyone, labor organizers, unions, community activists, peace activists, public service workers, intellectuals, artists, and writers who came before you (from Maryland or wherever). But those things that were good, those people who were good, who greeted you when you showed up, they worked for all that. Timberg writes (in the July 2015 *L.A. Magazine*), "In older, more settled places, you've missed your chance to belong if you weren't born there, but L.A. is different. You typically become a local a year or two after landing." But Timberg demonstrates nothing beyond a superficial idea of community, nothing more "local" than a list of tourist activities that he enjoyed about the city ("Rhino Records... Canter's... Largo... We hiked in Joshua Tree, drove to remote, tree-shaded wineries..."). After "landing," these "middle class" writers or artists live the detached life of tourists who want a life served to them by the community. They want no part of the struggle to make that community.

It may be that you as writer or artist of the post-Reagan era do not have that privilege.

After the Reagonomic destruction of the "middle class," reducing many citizens to the "third-class" status where the rest of us always already were, fighting for our lives, I suggest that disregard of the issues, struggles, and history of the community is NOT in your interest as a human being ("the impossibility of being human," as Charles Bukowski put it), as a writer or artist, or as a citizen of any community.

Listen to the snide, complacent class disdain latent in the praise for Los Angeles in a source quoted in Timberg's article: "Siobhan Spain, who resettled in the Midwest when the Chinatown gallery she directed shut down, remembers L.A. as a magical place: 'Where else, on any certain day, could you witness Esa-Pekka Salonen conducting at Walt Disney Concert Hall, walk by a homeless person defecating on the sidewalk, swim near dolphins at Point Dume State Beach, help install artwork by Stanford Biggers, sit in traffic for over an hour, watch your friend act in an episode of *Nip/Tuck,* and go to sleep with ghetto birds circling your neighborhood?'" It's the magical white L.A., where you have friends working in "the industry" and Disney Concert Hall (magically built on top of the destroyed neighborhood of former Bunker Hill) and Point Dume State Beach are there for you; and it's not your friends "defecating on the sidewalk," not your people targeted by "ghetto birds." It's magical white L.A. until your gallery is shuttered and you are proletarianized. Ah, then it's not so "magical." Time to flee.

You, young artist, young writer. Go anywhere you like. But know that a community was there before you—this land was not a magically unpeopled wilderness to be colonized but a place of history, secrets, struggles, heroes, and issues. What made it a community was not magic, but labor. Maybe if your labor and your work relates to them, if your aesthetic process is open to that community, your work will not be superfluous. Your work might be useful. You may not have to suddenly flee, like a tourist from the off-season. As an artist or writer anywhere, you'll need community to survive. Your community-building not only helps you survive, it helps you produce.

4. This argues against the artist or writer as tourist, as parachute journalist. You can develop more organic sources.

5. Your own aesthetic process is a transformative activity; it's not an economic transaction that you purchase with a university degree.

6. See also, "Letter to a Young Nonprivileged Poet" by Sandra Simonds, http://blog.bestamericanpoetry.com/the_best_american_poetry/2015/06/advice-to-a-young-nonprivileged-poet-by-sandra-simonds.html

7. See also, "Writing the Truth: the Five Difficulties" by Bertolt Brecht, http://ricardo.ecn.wfu.edu/~cottrell/ope/archive/0903/att-0196/fiveDifficulties_brecht.pdf. In fact, there's probably a long list of interesting, useful ideas for you, too long to list here. Part of the fun is getting together with others to find it and discuss it.

8. You gotta have fun doing it. Too much fun.

9. Otherwise this is too much work.

Epilogue

The Pelicans by AP photographer Charlie Riedel

1.

They fly low, slung along a horizontal line of thought. At least they used
to. How lucky do you feel today? I saw them rise, one after the other,
arrive at a height and dive into the water. The sun rolled through cool
cloud cover. It wasn't emerging any way complete.

2.

On the drive to drop his child off at school, the radio related this certain
news item. As he glanced up from his coffee at the café, his cousin
talking about the economy, he caught a glimpse of a TV news anchor
with a certain image related to this news item emblazoned on a wide
screen. Driving Hollywood Blvd east toward the freeway, instead of the
souvenir t-shirt shops and tourists, instead of the sportswear billboard,
an image came to him. It took a trip around the block outside the coffee
shop to locate a parking space.

3.

I strike the existential mode, you lean to the essentialist, with stylish
lifestyle gestures. I hanker to caress quotidian notes while you go off
beyond the horizon. Yet there you are still, I would remind you. It
doesn't matter, you assert, you have the look of hard-won endurance in
your spleen and soul. What is it that we are drinking, that surrounds us,
this coffee?

4.

A teacher complained about a student. Another complained about
the administrator who many seemed to dislike for an abrasive voice
and pronounced indifference. A couple of students complained about
various lacks of the latest issue of the school newspaper. Somebody
complained that the latest round of budget cuts caused the district
to cancel all recycling programs, yet the district produced massive
amounts of paper waste. A bus driver cracked acerbically about another
driver who had taken his usual spot. That was as far as he was going with
the grievance at this time.

5.

I would speak to you. I would detain you on your way and speak to you. It's all a rush pell-mell to get from point A to point B, and when we get there, we may be well and dead. As we go the distance, I would detain you. The moment was, or will be, illuminated by light in the sky.

6.

Man on the sidewalk sticks out his tongue; every passerby who puts a quarter on his tongue can view the man swallow the coin, and, in an obvious, conditioned reflex, punch himself with terrific fury in the face as hard as he can. After ingesting a full day's work, he can collect himself off the concrete and make his way off across a parking lot.

7.

More than 170, 000 men, women, and children are in prison or jail in California. The United States, with 5% of the world's population, imprisons 23% of the world's prisoners. Somebody's out there looking for somebody to kill. Marine platoons go house to house in Iraq. In Afghanistan, the sons and grandsons of men funded, armed, and supplied by the CIA plant shells in the highways. Entire blocks of neighborhoods of New Orleans, Detroit, and other cities are destroyed or abandoned houses. The "transient" who killed the teenager was caught with his arm around her neck on an ATM video. One third of air strikes by unmanned predator drones in Iraq, Afghanistan, Somalia, Pakistan, and Yemen are estimated to kill civilians. These drones are "piloted" by people at facilities outside of Las Vegas, NV. It may not be apparent yet, but this picture is on fire at the margins.

8.

The monk's hoods of automobile front ends meditating upon us. Cabover semi-trailer trucks. Containerization (or containerisation) is a system of intermodal freight transport using standard intermodal containers as prescribed by the International Organization for Standardization (ISO). In Laurel Canyon, where I picked them up at Esme's house, I told the girls that the front of the "Country Store" used to be scrawled with psychedelic flowers, peace signs, and filigree in primary colors, and (according to blogs) was around the corner from

Jim Morrison of the Doors' house. After dropping Ruby in Highland Park, an older gent in lurid fluorescent yellow peddled across our lane, cutting us off on his reclining bicycle with mirror dangling on an extended armature from his helmet. My daughter complained about his get-up, his presumption of our lane in the public road. I said that our larger engine, all these engines surrounding us in the traffic stream, didn't remove his right as a human being to a place in traffic. "Bikers have rights too," I said. "Cars have to share the road. The world doesn't belong to them."

9.
The animal is there before you, covered with loathsome, reeking tar. You know that if you reach out and grab it, it will become alarmed and react with who knows what alarming reflexive strength and speed, survival instinct causing it to respond to your grip and presence with what awkward horrid movement, gawky, flopping, filth-spattering thrashing about. It is exhausted and likely to die on this spot, this animal.

Who wants to prevent the fishes in the sea from getting wet? And the suffering themselves share this callousness towards themselves and are lacking in kindness towards themselves. It is terrible that human beings so easily put up with existing conditions, not only with the sufferings of strangers but also with their own. All those who have thought about the bad state of things refuse to appeal to the compassion of one group of people for another. But the compassion of the oppressed for the oppressed is indispensable. It is the world's one hope.
—Bertolt Brecht

10.
What roads and highways have you in your long leg bones. What rain and winds have you in your tangled hairs and curls in your ears. What ranges of temperature, frost on granite and poppies blooming in the highway median, in your hapless attitudes. What voices and memories of voices in your misty DNA and DNA saliva. What bodies, what California, what coastlines do you take in stride in your walk, in your arrivals. What atmospheric shadows, what thunderheads rolling across the terrain, what discoloration swirling in the liquid, in amber

distillation of words. You didn't make this language of conquerors, English. With its bits, avocado, tableau, tyranny, chokolatl, crusted on your lips. I am looking at your mouth to see what you will say.

11.
We have a situation here. Someone runs off. Empty hallways, later on, empty hallways. I stepped between the guys who were fighting, somebody pulled one of them off the other. I pushed another one up against the wall. His face was blanched, his stare hollowed out with adrenaline, he was breathing hard. I don't know what was happening behind me. I turned and they were gone. He had his hand to his face, blood streaming from his nose. Blood drips on the floor. "Come on, let's go downstairs," I said. I took him by the arm, and he followed meekly, holding his nose. "Jesus, you're getting blood all over," somebody else said, leading another teen by the arm. We put them both in the elevator. "Are you okay?" the other guy asked his charge. His eyes were glassy, blood on his mouth, but he asserted, "Okay." When we got out of the elevator, someone said, "Wow, you were so cool about this whole thing. You went right in there like you deal with this kind of thing every day." I didn't say how hard my heart was beating, how I flinched and tensed up immediately and hesitated till I saw an opening. Only then did I step in.

12.
I never thought I'd live to see some of these changes. That gives me some effulgent purplish feelings and tumescent impulses. Like Quitobaquito desert spring water welling up from the Organ Pipe Nat'l Monument landscape alongside the AZ/Mexico border, three strands of barbed wire north of Mexico, highway out of Sonoita. Three stars fell over the horizon, and they slaughtered all those Indians all over California. Who knows, who remembers, but that we might do something now. Who expected to be alive?

13.
All this bullshit creeps up on us. Our children look on us with suspicion, noting our discolorations, our aura of rainbowish encrudences, our fuming at the air. Silence compiles it; there's no hiding behind wordless boxes while it falls out of the air like petroleum bullshit. Walking around

shopping in Lower Manhattan in the used-to-be Village, in the used-to-be Soho, in the used-to-be, does not scrape off the accumulate muck. We're moving slower, we're getting wearier of the spike of sky. Time will come. Time will come! It has. They talk about this, they talk about that, but where was the money spent?

14.

I sent you a message, a card. Did you get it? Circumference of darkness with a line of lights, almost a ring. Vitality of night so much the larger for it. Center edge of aluminum and error. Wan steel of our habit. I had to say something urgent. It was about the moment and the opportunity. I had to presume on the basis of our shared correspondence, even if it was perhaps too much in the past for you, or seemingly so. Someone said you were dealing with your drug problem; and you yourself told me more than once you could barely take care of yourself, no way you'd ever be able to deal with "someone else's problems." But I was reminded of our visions before that, you know we appeared there, you and I. Now we're here. My messages were about that. I'll try to get in touch with you again, in some other way.

Thanks Again

Fried chicken smell of the past when Los Angeles was a blast of car horn, beer, particulate, urine in the corners—"Hey, Dad, we're talking about you!"—parking lots spilled into Beaudry, Temple, Beverly, First—the streets emptied into bars, puddled in street lights necklacing avenues and boulevards all the way to the surf. Eyes shining, faces flushed with ecstasy, that five-minute summary of five years. Who were you then? How did it happen? The city cooked the night. The ocean breathed. Little fish died like eyelids. They swam through your dreams, fishes and eyelids, like cars streaming the 5 freeway, and when you awoke, the fishes and eyelids desiccated, hanging in salty bags all the way from the South Pacific to Ranch 99 Market. I saw everyone who was nothing like you, but the time reference was off. Faces flipped like cards. You felt forgotten. Women made beautiful babies with the industry of cars, ships, planes. Crashes occurred. Indexes of leftover lives collated with indices of plywood partitions, statistical margins, self-delusion with a rasp of crows. They were missing you but would forget all about it. Give us this day, this day of petroleum. The historical moment aligned like cans on shelves of family markets throughout Southern Calif. Rusty pile of cans in a desertscape, the way a horny toad gives you the eye. All the wild motion of sky goes on and on. We go on, coated in the particulate, in lungs and tears, our tongues and cavities, wear buildings like worn-out ideologies, wear worn-out ideologies like sunshine divided into columns. Fried chicken smell of summer afternoons, summer nights all winter long. Fried chicken smell of dad's ghost, the one he shadowed wherever he walked. Fried chicken smell of downtown L.A. SRO hotel hallways, murphy beds, Bunker Hill. I was talking to you. Whatever you had said drew a finger across it, left this smudge pointing the direction you'd gone.

INDEX BY TITLE

Epilogue

ACKNOWLEDGEMENTS

Thanks to the editors of publications where some of these appeared: *Angel City Review, Best American Experimental Writing 2015, CultureStr/ke, La Bloga, Lana Turner Journal, Los Angeles Review of Books, Ping Pong, Poetry Foundation Blog, Párrafo, The L.A. Telephone Book, Vol. 1*, and *The Poetry Loft*.

The quote by Bertolt Brecht on page 211 comes from "The World's One Hope," *Bertolt Brecht Poems 1913–1956*, edited by John Willet and Ralph Manheim, with Erich Fried, 1976, New York: Methuen, Inc.

Thanks again to everyone, to our families, friends and collaborators, especially Arturo Romo, Karen Yamashita, Ruth Hsu, Ben Ehrenreich, Lisa Chen, Andy Hsiao, Brent Armendinger, Randy Cauthen, Mike Sonksen, Juan Felipe Herrera, Chiwan Choi, Peter Woods, Jessica Ceballos Campbell, E. Tammy Kim, Sunyoung Lee, Neelanjana Banerjee, Sean Deyoe, and Douglas Kearney, as well as the late Wanda Coleman and Austin Straus.

Poet, teacher, and community activist Sesshu Foster was born in 1957 and raised in East Los Angeles. He earned his MFA from the Iowa Writers' Workshop and returned to L.A. to continue teaching, writing, and community organizing. *City Terrace Field Manual*, a collection of prose poetry, was published by Kaya Press in 1997. His third collection of poetry, *World Ball Notebook* (2009), won an American Book Award and an Asian American Literary Award for Poetry. Foster is also the author of the speculative-fiction novel *Atomik Aztex* (2005), which won the Believer Book Award.